Perseverance

An Alaskan's 2,000 mile journey
on the Appalachian Trail

BILL JACK

Jeannie
I so admire your
life and how you have
touched so many people
/ God Bless

PO Box 221974 Anchorage, Alaska 99522-1974
books@publicationconsultants.com, www.publicationconsultants.com

Bill Jack

ISBN Number: 978-1-59433-877-9
eBook ISBN Number: 978-1-59433-878-6
Library of Congress Catalog Card Number: 2019905754

Manufactured in the United States of America

Dedication

I dedicate this book to my wife, Penny. She has been my partner for over 45 years. She has encouraged me, stood beside me, backed me, inspired me, helped mold me, and, yes, has never hesitated to speak her mind when I needed a scolding. She has been a loving mother. Our grandkids call her Yayaa and love her to death. She crafts, knits, and creates beautiful skin-sewing garments. She is a very generous person, gifting away much of what she makes. I am very proud of her. I am thankful for her love, friendship, loyalty, kindness, and especially her patience with me. I am thankful for all that she does. She is my best friend, my soul mate, and the love of my life.

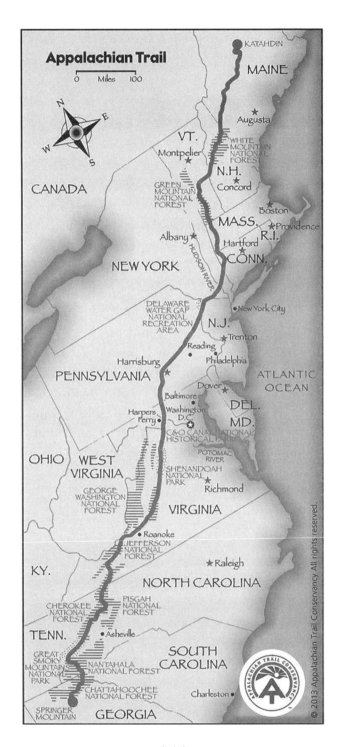

Foreword

by Shawn R. Lyons
Acknowledged Alaska Hiking Authority

Many decades have passed since I hiked the 2,100-plus-mile Appalachian Trail in the summer of 1972—the 104th person to do so. One would think that the memories would have faded. But many haven't. In *Perseverence*, 70-plus-year-old Bill Jack's memoirs of hiking this same trail, brings back even more of those memories.

While *Perseverence* makes evident how many things along the trail remain the same, it also makes evident how many things have changed. Sometimes, 5 or 6 days would pass before I met another hiker. In contrast, Bill hiked many a mile in the company of many others and his book tells of no bad word passing amongst them. They certainly cursed the sleet, wind, rain, and snow at times—as hikers most everywhere will do—but never at each other.

To those who have not hiked the Appalachian Trail this will seem extraordinary, even unbelievable. Those who have hiked the trail, though, will nod knowingly at this camaraderie. In telling of the people he met, Bill introduces the non-hiker to this exceptionally high number of hikers sharing battering storms, steep climbs, and earned rests. We could all take a lesson from their sense of commitment and devotion to a thin trail stretching for 2,100-plus miles up the east coast of a continent.

All these people hiking north and south and back and forth for a few days or a whole season has, in turn, resulted in another change—the creation of a large Appalachian Trail cottage industry. One can now find many more cabins, huts, and shelters along the trail; many more hotels, motels, hostels and restaurants just off the trail; many more shuttles; and many more stores supplying food and equipment hikers truly need.

This brings us to the book's title: *Perseverence* — an appropriate title. Despite all the new luxuries along the trail, it still takes perseverance to hike it, as every hiker who ever completed it well knows. It seems probable, though no records exist, that every person who ever completed this trail thought at some time or another about quitting and heading for home. My moment came in southern Pennsylvania with 1,000 miles behind me and 1,000-plus miles still to go and the rain falling heavily.

Bill tells of another aspect of perseverance. The perseverance it takes to return again and again from year to year requires renewing that commitment with every new beginning. To one who hiked the trail in a single outing, those hiking the trail in many outings over many years make even more of a commitment.

Bill had to renew this commitment seven times over the course of three years—and most, not out of choice, but because of injuries, forced him off the trail. The sheer effort to travel back and forth from his home in Alaska and begin again and again seems a true act of will. Eventually, though—after 170 days hiking, with 20 rest days, over three years of time—Bill finished his memorable commitment.

An additional bit of perseverance led to penning of this book. For those who have hiked the trail this book will bring back many vivid memories of their own experiences on the trail. For this reader, these white-blazed trail markers leading across the crest of Fontana Dam or down the main thoroughfares of Hot Springs and Damascus; rhododendrons blanketing Mount Rogers in southern Virginia; winding back and forth across the Blue Ridge Parkway in Northern Virginia; climbing of Bear Mountain in New York and its view to the south of the New York City skyline; the hushed grounds of Graymoor Monastery; the loud playing fields of Dartmouth College; above-the-clouds hike along the South Presidential Range between the Mitzpah Hut to Lakes of the Clouds Hut; the ford across the Kennebec River in central Maine; and finally, climbing to the summit Mount Katahdin. The wind-battered sign marking the finish, seems to look out over all of Maine.

Thus, the Appalachian Trail may have changed in kind but not in essence. One certainly finds far more people making their way along the trail, but that only makes the trail family larger. For those who have not hiked the trail, perhaps Bill's memories will inspire them to hike it or possibly attempt a new adventure of their own.

Holcomb—My Trail Name

Trail names became popular in the 1970s. It was easier to remember other hikers by a nickname. In addition, taking a trail name somewhat signifies leaving the hassles of everyday life and acquiring a new name for this different life of hiking. Some hikers choose their own before they even start the trail. A trail name may be based on where a hiker is from or what that hiker did as a career. Most hikers wait to be dubbed by other hikers on the trail. A hiker's trail name may come from a personality trait, some gear the hiker is carrying or possibly something the hiker did on the trail. Usually you never find out the hiker's real name. I have mentioned many hikers by their trail name throughout this book. Following are a few more that I encountered: Smoky, Roadrunner, Christmas Tree, Trouble, Flash, Bonnie and Clyde, Carrots, Cookie, Disco, Whiskers, Sunflower, Blueberry, Nibbles, Cocoa, Waffles, Cellphone and Smoothie. I decided my trail name would be in memory of a good friend of 40 years. Jim Holcomb was hiking near his home in Sisters, Oregon, in the beginning of 2015, when his heart suddenly stopped working. Jim loved the outdoors, was in excellent shape, and was an avid hiker. He was a devoted and loving father and husband. He was a kind and generous friend to many. Many years ago, Jim and his wife, Jeannie, showed up at our doorstep in Anchorage, Alaska. They had flown in from their home in Oregon with their bicycles and camping gear, ready for a

2000-mile bicycle trip down the Alcan Highway. After a couple of days of final preparations, they mounted their bikes, and Jeannie looked up at Jim and said, "Let's go, Holcomb." I asked Jeannie if I could honor Jim with Holcomb as my trail name. She said Jim was intrigued with trail names and to definitely take the name.

Introduction

The Appalachian Trail now travels approximately 2180 continuous miles through the Appalachian Mountains. It all started as a vision of a long distant trail, from Benton MacKaye, way back in the 1920's. Early in the 1930's, Myron Avery, an avid hiker, started mapping out the trail. He convinced many hiking clubs to help blaze the path and oversaw most of the 2000 mile construction process. Avery was from Maine and insisted that the trail end at the 5000 foot Mount Katahdin in northern Maine. By the time it was officially finished on August 14, 1937, he had hiked the entire distance.

It was designed to be a very difficult trail so that it would challenge the most experienced hikers. It travels through 14 Eastern states and requires constant climbing and descending over very tough mountain terrain. It was not that popular in the early years, but today more than a million hikers will hike some portion of the trail each year. These Appalachian Mountains are some of the oldest mountains in the world and the surrounding areas of the 2180 miles of trail, is filled with American history.

Contents

CHAPTER 1

Georgia

> "The only impossible journey is the one you never begin."
> —Anthony Robbins

My wife, Penny, would burst out laughing night after night as she read this particular book in bed before going to sleep. I would ask her what was so funny, and when she could finally talk, she would read me a couple of lines and start laughing again. She was reading *A Walk in the Woods*, a book by Bill Bryson about his hiking experiences on the Appalachian Trail. I am always game for a laugh, so I decided that when she finished the book, I would give it a go.

After completing the book, Bryson somehow, through his humor, had me believing that the fun I had reading his book would translate to having as much fun hiking the trail. My desire to hike the Appalachian Trail (AT) increased, and eventually I became obsessed about it. Bryson had put a spell on me. You might say I was a little naive, not realizing at the time that I had picked one of the most difficult long-distance hiking trails in the world for my first long-distance hike. Little did I know.

Since we were both retired, I suggested to Penny that we should hike the Appalachian Trail together. She said yes, but

I started realizing she wasn't as serious about it as I was. After weeks of pondering and wondering if I should really attempt this adventure, I decided that at my age, if I did not make a move soon, it may be too late in a few years. Penny responded with mixed emotions. I often talked about doing things without ever following through. She kind of believed that this monumental adventure was just a pipe dream of mine.

The next few months I started training by hiking around the hills of Anchorage. In the evenings, I found myself checking out hikers' blogs who had hiked the AT. Some hikers had provided videos online displaying all their gear. I started making weekly trips to REI, checking out sleeping bags, hiking shoes, tents, and asking lots of questions.

One day I came home from REI with a backpack weighing five pounds, big enough to hold 50 pounds of gear. I think REI wants customers to buy a large backpack so they can buy more of their stuff to fill it up. Penny was a little bit exasperated when I told her the Price. She had not really given me her blessings about what I was planning. After several weeks, she started to realize that this nonsense of mine might actually become a reality. I think she thought my life might be in danger and started taking more interest and offering me advice from her many winter camping experiences.

I have always been kind of a tight wad with money and was always looking for a bargain. I started accumulating a bunch of discounted gear, not really paying attention to how much each item weighed. One of the bargains was a tent that I found for just $59. I came home and started setting it up in the living room. There were no instructions. Penny sat there on the couch, shaking her head as I struggled to figure out how everything went together. She watched with interest and showed great patience, allowing me to figure it out myself. Finally I finished, climbed in, and laid down. I was glad she had not videoed the first setup.

After accumulating an enormous amount of gear, I loaded and reloaded my backpack at least a dozen times. To be honest, this was a huge unknown to this 70 -year-old novice hiker. It was all a little overwhelming to think about. I started to get more than a little nervous as my departure time grew close. Hiking solo only increased my anxiety. I could hardly sleep at night. I tried to act calm around my wife, but she was obviously not being fooled.

Before I could have a nervous breakdown, I soon decided to head to Georgia the end of February 2015. My wife and kids immediately objected. They repeated to me many times, "Why go so early?" I immediately reminded them that Georgia was a lot warmer than Anchorage, Alaska, this time of year. I made my flight and lodging arrangements.

On February 25, 2015, I flew on Alaska Airlines from Anchorage to Atlanta. I was relieved to find my backpack at the baggage area. After grabbing it, I hustled over to the MARTA train station, which was conveniently located next to the baggage claim area. I took the train through Atlanta and then on to the farthest North Terminal.

Hiker Hostel was owned by Josh and Leigh Saint, who were former AT thru-hikers. They picked hikers up at this station and transported them to their hostel in Dahlonega, Georgia. Josh was soon there to pick me up and, during the hour drive, showed great patience answering many of my questions, which I am sure he had answered a thousand times before. After arriving, I found 20 hikers already settled in for the night. The hostel was well kept, and house rules required lights out at 10:30 p.m.

The next morning, the hosts served a hearty buffet breakfast of scrambled eggs, sausage, oatmeal, toast, juice, and coffee. We were all excited but also a little nervous about the trek we had all committed to. After packing up, the three vans started shuttling hikers to four different trailheads. There were six of us, all solo hikers, who were shuttled to the base of Springer

Mountain. Most thru-hikers come to the trail as solo hikers. I was told that after a few weeks, a hiker usually finds someone who hikes their pace and end up spending many days and nights hiking and camping together.

It was a good 30-minute drive up a narrow twisting dirt road that got us within a mile of the top of Springer Mountain, the official starting point of the Appalachian Trail. As we ascended the road, I wasn't having a panic attack, but it was close. I tried to calm myself by imagining that the six of us were on this mission together.

Soon we arrived at the trailhead parking lot and climbed out of the van and put on our backpacks. The driver took some pictures of us together and wished us all a safe journey. As we started climbing, the anxiety disappeared, and the hike became fun.

At mile zero, we were experiencing much excitement and anticipation for trail ahead.

We reached the top in about 30 minutes to find a large boulder in the woods with a plate on it that indicated the starting point of our great adventure. At this point, all of us took our packs off and started taking pictures, which seemed to be a spontaneous reaction for everyone. It was exciting, and we were all pumped up by the significance of the moment.

After about 15 minutes, we swung our backpacks on and began our descent. The temperature was about 35 degrees as we hiked down the trail under cloudy skies. We took several breaks together that day, and all but one of the group, hiked a total of nine miles to Hawk Mountain Shelter for the night.

Unfortunately, Mingle, one of the hikers in our group, had to be rescued six miles into the hike due to dizziness. He had been struggling up the mountains and out of breath all day. Two miles before the shelter, he could not go any further. Two hikers in our group helped him into his sleeping bag and called for help. The rescue team came up another nearby trail in a four-wheel-drive rescue vehicle and transported him to a hospital. Two days later, we were informed and relieved that he was just out of shape and had been released after a night's stay in the hospital. This reminded me of Josh at Hiker Hostel telling me that 20 percent of thru-hikers quit after the first 30 miles. Those hikers were usually inexperienced and had not trained properly for the demands this trail requires.

I set up my tent next to the Hawk Mountain Shelter and laid out my pad, sleeping bag, and supplies inside the tent. I took my stove and food bag and went over to the three-sided shelter and cooked a Mountain House beef stew dinner. There were seven hikers tenting and three others planning to sleep in the shelter. The temperature dropped, and it started snowing. I exclaimed to myself, "Are you kidding me? This is Georgia."

As darkness descended on us, I crawled into my tent and put on my warmest clothes. I slipped into my sleeping bag, pulling it up over my head. It was so cold that I did not dare fall asleep, thinking I might freeze to death. I wiggled my toes, tried curling into the embryo position, but ended up tossing and turning all night. Finally around 7:00 a.m., I crawled out of my sleeping bag and put on my warmest hiking clothes. After putting on my shoes, I climbed out of the tent to find ten inches of snow on the ground. I asked myself, "What have I got myself into?"

I broke a path 100 yards through the deep snow down to the water source to fill my water bottle. By the time I got back, the three hikers who had slept in the shelter were slowly climbing out of their sleeping bags. One asked me if it was warmer sleeping in my tent than in the shelter. I told him I shivered and shook all night long but thought it might have been warmer in the shelter, as I heard a lot of snoring from there.

I got my stove going on the shelter floor to boil some water for oatmeal. I kept moving around to stay warm. The hot oatmeal helped to slow my shivering. Next, I was introduced to the process of thawing my frozen metal tent poles with my bare hands so I could fold them up. As my tent collapsed onto the snow, I realized I still had some gear inside my tent. Without filling my backpack with too much snow, I was able to get the rest of my gear out of the tent and into my pack. It took me two hours to break camp and pack up. I was totally out of my comfort zone.

Three hikers had already left about 20 minutes before my departure. After slowly following their tracks through the heavy wet snow for about three miles, I saw them ahead breaking trail up the steep Sassafras Mountain. I eventually caught up to them as they were taking a break. I decided it was my turn to break trail.

For the next four miles, I struggled carrying my 40-pound pack up the mountains and through the deep snow. A young married couple from Virginia caught up with me as we climbed Justus Mountain. They were in good spirits and glad to take a turn breaking trail the last two miles into Gooch Mountain Shelter.

Shortly after I arrived there, hikers started arriving one by one. We tried to get a fire going right in front of the shelter, but it was a meager one, since it was virtually impossible to find any wood under the ten inches of snow. Eventually a total of eight hikers arrived before nightfall. Knowing that heat rises, I decided to climb up and sleep on the upper deck of the shelter. Four hikers stayed in the lower deck, and I was hoping the body heat from below would make the upper deck a little warmer. Wishful thinking.

I put two pair of dry socks on along with my warmest clothes and crawled into my 30-degree sleeping bag. The temperature was in the mid-20s, and I again tossed and turned all night to stay warm. I was a little scared of my predicament, but felt some comfort in the fact that I was with hikers in the same quandary.

The next day, I was up at daybreak. It was a struggle to put on my frozen shoes. I again cooked oatmeal, and since I didn't have to pack up my tent, it only took me an hour and a half to hit the trail. The goal was to hike 12 miles to Woods Hole Shelter. It was a bit easier hike through the snow, since the trail had been broken in by the previous day's hikers. I arrived just before it got dark to find only three hikers already in their sleeping bags for the night. After cooking, I put on my last two pair of dry socks and my warmest clothes again. I elected to stay in the shelter and was in my sleeping bag by 8:00 p.m.

The next morning, I was up at daybreak and anxious to get to Mountain Crossings Hostel, only four miles away. I ate a protein bar for breakfast and was soon hiking. My thermometer, attached to my backpack, showed it was 20 degrees. The chill factor was much lower because the freezing wind was brutal. I had to keep moving to stay warm. At the top of Blood Mountain, Zack, a hiker with whom I had camped the past two nights, caught up with me. After a short break, we carefully maneuvered over some very slippery ledges, coming down the 1500-foot decent. The hostel, one of the oldest on the AT, was a welcome site. I registered for a night's stay, took a hot shower, did laundry, and quenched my thirst with several soda pops. The complex had a well-stocked outfitter store. Someone was thoughtfully cooking hot dogs outside for hikers. Zack and I each devoured at least six of them. Since I had not slept well the past three nights, I decided to take a nap in the nice warm bunkhouse.

After about two hours in the comfort of my sleeping bag, my feet started throbbing. I got up to find them enormously swollen. I suddenly realized that I had frostbitten my feet. It was difficult to walk, so I decided to get back to Alaska, where they knew how to deal with frostbite. I was embarrassed and devastated.

After only four days of hiking 30 miles on the Appalachian Trail, I had to call it quits. I hired a shuttle to drive me to the North Spring MARTA train station. The train took about an hour to get to the Atlanta Airport. I boarded an Alaska Airlines plane to Anchorage through Seattle. Arriving in Anchorage on March 2, my wife, Penny, took me to the emergency room at Providence Hospital. My feet looked really bad, and I was really worried about toes having to be amputated.

While teaching school in Nome, Alaska, from 1982 to 1998, Penny and I raised and raced sled dogs. In 1991 and 1992, I ran the 1049 Iditarod Sled Dog Race. Each year, the temperatures dipped to minus 40 degrees during the race, but I never suffered from frostbite until I went to Georgia to hike the Appalachian Trail.

The doctor put me on 800 mg of ibuprofen every eight hours. He told me to take warm footbaths twice a day and to keep my feet elevated. In a couple of days, the swelling went down, but I continued the footbaths for several more days. I had lost feeling in my two largest toes on each foot.

After two weeks, I went to a frostbite specialist, and they were pleased with the circulation in all of my toes. I did a few hikes in the Anchorage area, and my feet held up fine. Three weeks after leaving the trail, I decided to go back to the Mountain Crossings Hostel and continue my trek northbound. My wife and kids naturally objected.

CHAPTER 2

Georgia-Tennessee-North Carolina

"Into the forest I go, to lose my mind and find my soul."
—John Meir

On March 19, 2015, after flying into Atlanta, I again took the MARTA train to the last station north of Atlanta. This time I arranged a shuttle to Neel Gap and began hiking on March 20. This late in March, the temperature was in the 50s, the snow had disappeared, and there were many more hikers moving up the trail. At the outfitter store, I bought a few snacks and a sports drink to take with me; I decided to hike six miles up the AT to a campsite on top of Wildcat Mountain.

After setting my tent up, it started raining, so I immediately crawled in and retired for the night. By morning, the rain had stopped, but everything was damp. After packing up, I took my time and hiked 12 miles to Blue Mountain Shelter. There were several hikers there tenting, and some staying in the shelter.

At 7:00 p.m., Phantom, a former air-force fighter pilot, hiked in and set up his tent close to mine. He was sitting on a log eating his dinner, so I went over to visit with him. He had hiked an impressive eighteen miles from Neel Gap. We both seemed to enjoy each other's company after hiking alone all day.

Bullet and his dad, Magnum, showed up. Bullet erected his hammock between two trees with an enormous rain fly, four feet above the hammock. The unique setup drew a lot of attention from the surrounding campers. Some hikers sleep in the three-sided shelters, many sleep in their tents, and some also in hammocks strung across two trees.

A hiker sees new hikers every day. Most of the time, hikers are very friendly. They respect one another for enduring the same strenuous hikes day after day and, many times, become instant friends. A hiker usually hikes alone but often stops and takes a snack or a lunch break with others. Campsites and shelters become popular gathering spots after 4:00 p.m. Campfires are often started that draw hikers in to warm up and visit. Hikers are also busy at this time cooking, setting up camp, and checking their AT guides, many times discussing the next day's hike. The AT provides a very special and unique social life that hikers enjoy and treasure. Just being out there creates camaraderie.

It was March 22; I started hiking down Blue Mountain at 7:00 a.m. I noticed a lot of hikers would eat a couple of bars for breakfast and hit the trail. I decided to do the same and save an unnecessary 30 to 40 minutes of cooking every morning.

After hiking over Rocky Mountain, I descended 3000 feet down to Indian Grave Gap. Some students on spring break from the University of Georgia were there with water, strawberries, cookies, brownies, hot dogs, and lounge chairs. People providing refreshments (trail magic) to hikers at road crossings are referred to as trail angels. Many times the trail angels turn out to be former hikers of the AT. A hiker never knows where trail magic is waiting, but it is always a very pleasant surprise.

After heaping the trail angels with abundant thanks, I climbed up to the summit of Tray Mountain at 4200 feet. Phantom had hiked on to a campsite another five miles up the trail. I decided to tent there at the Tray Mountain campsite. It rained all night. I did not sleep well and, at 4:00 a.m., decided to pack up. Being so inexperienced, my stuff got wet packing up in the rain. This meant I was carrying an extra five pounds of wet gear.

After hiking eleven miles into Dick's Creek Gap at mile 70, I hitched a ride into Hiawassee, Georgia, and registered for one night at the Holiday Inn. I had to dry out my gear and try and get better organized. I spread out my tent in my room to dry and did laundry. I felt a little light-headed, probably due to dehydration, so I headed to the grocery store down the street. At the sandwich shop, I ordered a ham-and-cheese sub loaded with vegetables. As I ate and drank a sports drink at their sit-down area, I started to feel much better.

Later that day, I ran into Phantom in the lobby of the hotel. We decided to meet for the complimentary breakfast the next morning and afterward share a shuttle back to the trail at 8:00 a.m. That evening, I enjoyed another meal at a buffet restaurant next door.

Seven miles into the hike the next day, I left Georgia and entered into North Carolina at mile 77. I continued hiking ten more miles and reached Standing Indian Shelter at 8:00 p.m. The 17-mile hike was a confidence booster, since it was my longest hike so far. About 30 hikers were already settled in for the night. I recognized and acknowledged Phantom, Magnum, and Bullet, but all the others were new faces. I set up my tent and then boiled water for a lasagna dinner in the dark. I hit the hay around 9:00 p.m. The next morning I broke camp and was first out of the campsite shortly after daybreak.

It was a much easier 20-mile trail to Rock Gap Shelter. The camping area was very crowded, and some hikers graciously invited me to share some pizza and soda pop with them. The pizza had been delivered to them from the town of Franklin.

I decided to set up my tent down the hill from the shelter where Magnum and Bullet had a campfire going. This father-son team had been passing by me each day for the past 60 miles. As I ate my beef stew dinner by the campfire, Magnum explained to me that they were going to skip going into Franklin the next day and planned a two-day hike into Nantahala Outdoor Center. When I got back to my tent, I did an inventory of my food and decided I had enough grub to do the same. By skipping the town of Franklin, we would be passing about 50 hikers who were there or headed there.

The next day, I hiked another 20 miles, arriving at Cold Spring Shelter at 6:00 p.m. at mile 125. There were five thru-hikers at this shelter, whom I had never seen before: Obsolete, Caboose, Ox, Sherb, and Honey Bee. Sherb informed me that he had his tent set up on a flat area, 75 feet above where the shelter was located. I hiked up to the ridge and decided to do the same. I was glad it was calm, because a strong wind might have had us tumbling off the ridgeline and down the cliffs below.

Sherb had just graduated from high school in Massachusetts. He came from a hiking family, was very mature for his age, and was a delightful young man. After setting up my tent, I boiled water for a Mountain House teriyaki chicken dinner. After mixing it together, I took it down to the shelter to visit with the others and eat by the campfire.

It was dark soon, so Sherb and I, with the help of our headlamps, headed back up to our campsite. It was a starlit night. Arriving at our tents, we turned our headlamps off and stood on the ridgetop admiring the sparkling stars and the many lights across the valley far below. It was a peaceful way to end our day, and we soon retired to the comfort of our tents.

The next morning I left camp at 6:00 a.m., knowing it was a town day. There was only one big climb, and reaching the top, I took the wrong trail. This happened just as I was beginning to feel confident about hiking the Appalachian Trail. This wrong trail, luckily, ended up at the same spot at the bottom of the mountain where I had just come from. At that point, I did not realize I had taken the wrong trail. All of a sudden, here came the five hikers whom I had just camped with. I was totally turned around. They assured me they were going northbound. I then had to climb the same mountain that I had done an hour earlier. When I reached the top, Obsolete complimented me on my three miles of extra credit.

We all arrived at the recreational area at Nantahala Outdoor Center about 2:00 p.m. It is located right on the trail. The big attraction there was rafting down the Nantahala River. It is a huge complex, and I, along with other hikers, were disappointed to find that the bunkhouse and cabins were totally booked. There were no rooms, or any tent sites available, however, I was able to do laundry at their laundry room. I also enjoyed a hamburger and milkshake at their restaurant. After resupplying at their well-stocked outfitter store, I was ready to continue up the trail.

I decided to hike two miles up the next mountain to a campsite and pitch my tent. The temperature had dropped to 30 degrees. When I reached the campsite, Sherb, Honeybee, Clank, and five other hikers were there with a warm campfire going. After snacking and mingling around the fire, I hung my food bag over a high limb, which is usually a nightly affair. Most shelters have high poles and chains provided for hanging food bags to keep bears away from sleeping areas.

The next morning, we woke up to three inches of snow and a temperature of 25 degrees. I had warmer shoes this time around but was a little concerned about my feet. I hung around until all eight hikers had left, to make sure a good path had been worn down for me. It was a very long climb out of this campsite. After about an hour of hiking, Bullet went by me wearing gym shorts, moving like a rocket. His trail name was very appropriate. He goes up mountains like a cheetah. His dad was about ten minutes behind him, and was moving at a rapid pace as well.

At the top, there were some spectacular views looking far below at the Nantahala Outdoor Center. By noon, I was happy to see the snow had melted. At the end of the hike, there was a very steep 700-foot climb up Jacob's Ladder. It about did me in. Totally exhausted, I arrived at the Brown Fork Shelter. Already there were Numbers, Doc Holiday, Overload, August, and Happy, whom I had all hiked with earlier that day. They had a nice campfire going right in front of the shelter. I boiled water for some hot tea and a warm meal of hamburger pie.

The next day we woke up to a temperature of 20 degrees. It was tough crawling out of our warm sleeping bags. I put on two pairs of warm dry socks. We all hit the trail about 7:00 a.m., in a hurry to stay warm and get to Fontana Dam Lodge. As we descended, the temperature warmed, and we reached this popular oasis at 2:00 p.m.

The lodge was a couple of miles from the trail, but they offered free shuttles to and from their complex. Many hikers take a zero day there, before entering the Smoky Mountain National Park. A zero day means an extra day of rest. After 135 miles in eight days of hiking, I needed the extra rest and food, so I registered for two nights.

The Fontana Dam Lodge is a very large complex with a great restaurant, laundry facilities, a resupply store, and even a post office. There was also a very large Fontana Dam Shelter right on the trail known as the Hilton of all shelters for hikers on a budget. It was large, with a nice view and even had a shower for hikers.

After some great meals and a good rest for two days, I left Fontana Dam Lodge at 7:30 a.m. on March 31, with enough food for a five-day hike. I had enjoyed visiting with Bullet, Magnum, Sherb, Obsolete, Ox, Caboose, August, Doc Holiday, Numbers, Happy, and Phantom. Most of these hikers, including TJ, passed me later that day, but I was feeling good about my progress. I eventually joined them after a 16 -mile hike up some big climbs to a crowded Spence Field Shelter at 5000 feet.

There were many tents set up outside, and 15 of us were cramped into the two-decker shelter. Sherb was there along with Phantom. I met Fireweed for the first time. She informed me that she had worked for a few years in Alaska with the Bureau of Land Management. I assumed that is where she fell in love with the fireweed flower.

The next morning, TJ and I were up at 5:30, packing up outside the shelter, trying to be quiet so we didn't wake all the others who were still sleeping. TJ was a fast hiker and pulled ahead of me quickly as we left the campsite at 6:00 a.m. A little over a mile up the trail, I came to a peak called Rocky Top at 5440 feet. It was a beautiful morning. This area was out of the woods, which allowed for some magnificent views with fog patches covering a few areas far below. I stopped for several minutes to take it all in. A hiker named Doc caught up with me and took my picture at this special place.

I took my time today, taking several breaks and hiked a total of 14 miles to Double Spring Gap Shelter. I enjoyed visiting with Sherb and Fireweed as we sat on some benches eating dinner. There was good spring water coming out of a pipe at this mountain top shelter at 5500 feet. After I explained to Fireweed that hiking the Appalachian Trail was my first overnight hiking experience, she commented, "You have picked a pretty difficult trail to start your first long-distance hike." I replied, "I am finding that out the hard way."

Fireweed then looked at a large blister I was nursing on the bottom of my left foot. I was pretty much limping through the Smoky Mountain National Park. Fireweed advised me to get some toe sock liners that totally prevent blisters. Another lesson being learned the hard way.

I slept well in my tent and was up and hiking by 6:00 a.m. A park permit is required on your person to hike through the 70 miles of the Smoky Mountain National Park. There were many trails intersecting and joining the AT through the mountainous park as well. Many hikers staying at the shelters were actually hiking different trails. It was especially crowded this time of year in the park.

Three miles into the hike, I came to Clingmans Dome. At 6600 feet, it is the highest point on the Appalachian Trail. There were a couple of trails that went up to the Dome, and I somehow went in a half mile circle and was soon heading southbound. After about a mile of going the wrong way, I ran into Fireweed and Sherb. As soon as I saw them coming toward me, I shouted, "Not again."

The Appalachian Trail is well marked with painted white blazes, found on trees, boulders, and sometimes on rocks. You might think I would have recognized the trail I had just come up, but much of the woods look the same. The white blazes do not let you know whether you are going north or south. Sherb was also one of the hikers who had found me hiking southbound a few days before. He mentioned that he was becoming concerned about my sense of direction. I could tell by the expression on his face that he was thinking, *And this guy has 2000 more miles to go.*

Just before reaching Newfound Gap, a U.S. forest ranger coming down the trail stopped me and said, "I will see your permit now." They do check, and if a hiker doesn't have one, there is a heavy fine. I showed him my permit and was on my way.

Reaching Newfound Gap, a hiker crosses Route 441, the only road crossing through the 70 miles of the park. Hikers often find trail magic at this very large and popular parking lot. There is a couple from Florida who come here every year for their wedding anniversary to support hikers with food and drink.

After spending 20 minutes visiting with them, and eating and drinking my fill, they insisted I take more. They made me another sandwich to take and started stuffing my pockets with snacks and drinks. I had to stop up the trail to redistribute the snacks because my hiking shorts were falling down from the extra weight.

Many hikers hitch a ride 20 miles down to Gatlinburg, Tennessee, for town food and to spend the night at this very popular tourist town in the mountains. I have been told that if tourists see a hiker walking down the busy street, they will stare and sometimes stop the hiker to ask questions. I decided to avoid this out of the way detour and hike another three miles to the Icewater Spring Shelter.

Hikers are required to stay at the shelters throughout the Smoky Mountains National Park, due to so many bears and especially so many hikers. If a shelter is full, tenting is only allowed near the shelter. This time of year, the shelters were always full. In addition, there were usually 20 to 30 tents set up around the shelter.

The last shelter I stayed at in the Smoky National Park was Tricorner Knob Shelter at mile 223. It was a 13 -mile hike, and I arrived there at 1:30 in the afternoon. I was tempted to hike to the next shelter, eight miles down the trail, but instead found a spot in the lower shelf of the shelter. By nightfall, the 12-person capacity had reached 24 hikers packed inside. Many tents had been pitched around the shelter. Heavy rain was forecast, and, boy, did it rain. The noise on the tin roof of this horrendous downpour was deafening. The rain, the loud crackling thunder and bright lightning lasted about three hours. I did not sleep much, but it was good to be inside and dry.

The thunderstorm finally passed, and I could not sleep. I quietly moved all my stuff outside under a lean-to porch and started packing at 3:00 a.m. I noticed a stream of water was flowing right under TJ's tent nearby. I soon started hiking with my headlamp on. Much of the trail was filled with water, and the fog was very thick.

By 6:45 a.m., it was light enough to turn my dim headlamp off. It was a long descent and a very wet 18 -mile hike that included four tricky high-water crossings near the end. After a four-night, five-day hike through the Smoky National Park, I was glad that section was over. There was now more freedom to camp along the trail.

Hikers usually stay or stop for a resupply at the rustic Standing Bear Hostel after coming out of the park. The hostel has a bunkhouse, cabins for rent, a laundry, a sort of kitchen/dining area, a shower shack, an elevated privy shack, and a well-stocked store for hikers—a very unique place that every AT hiker should experience. Sharing stories in the bunkhouse that night at Standing Bear was TJ, Phantom, Obsolete, Caboose, Ox, Boomer and two others. There were other hikers tenting and enjoying some moonshine around a campfire. The Standing Bear Hostel was very welcoming and also had a hillbilly feel about the place.

At 5:00 a.m. in the bunkhouse, I was suddenly woken when something fuzzy jumped onto my neck. I hollered, "*A rat.*" as my arm frantically swept the creature onto the floor. Headlamps came on and revealed a cat, the hostel mascot, as it slowly walked away from my bunk. I meekly covered my head, and everyone went back to sleep.

I had been nursing and treating a very large blister on the bottom of my left foot all through the Smoky Mountains. I was not limping anymore, but I decided to give my foot a little more rest and did not leave until 11:30 a.m. Immediately after departing, there was a four-mile climb up Snowbird Mountain. After two miles of climbing, I stopped at a mountain stream for water. Bluegrass briefly stopped and asked me how much more of a climb was ahead. I told him we were only halfway up. He seemed surprised. Once I reached the top, I hiked two hundred yards down the trail along the ridgeline and found an inviting grassy campsite area. It was a perfect place to take a break. The sun was warm as I took off my pack, my shoes, and my socks. I wanted the sun to help heal the blister. As I laid down, I soon fell asleep.

Two hours later, I woke when two hikers decided this would be a good place to camp for the night. Halfway up the climb, the 50 -pound pack that his girlfriend was carrying was just too heavy for her, so he gallantly offered to carry her pack as well. Carrying her 50 -pound pack on his chest and his 50 -pound pack on his back, he literally collapsed right in front of me. It was 4:00 p.m.; I had overslept.

I thanked the couple for waking me up as they were setting up their massive tent. A thru-hiking German couple named Bud and Bud Light briefly stopped and soon continued on down the trail. I packed up and hiked six more miles. I set up my tent at Brown Gap at around mile 250. I noticed that Bud and Bud Light were camped about 100 yards up the trail. I cooked, ate, climbed into my tent, and was asleep by 7:30 p.m.

The next morning I was up at 5:00 a.m., anxious to hike 23 miles to Hot Springs. It was a beautiful day, and the trail was smooth as I climbed up to the summit of Match Patch at 4600 feet. I came to hikers named Skittles and Twiggy, who were still under their canopy at the summit. The wind was blowing about 20 mph. I stopped and

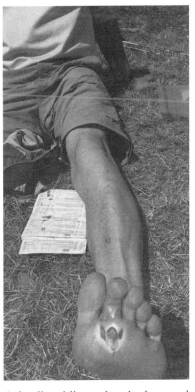

A healing blister that had caused much discomfort, limping the past 70 miles through the Smoky Mountains.

mentioned that I was glad to see the wind hadn't blown them away.

There were hundreds of acres of green grass that covered Match Patch. Many years ago it was all forest. The trees were cleared and logged to provide pasture for sheep and cattle. In 1982, the U.S. Forest Service purchased the land for the Appalachian Trail. The 360-degree view was spectacular.

Skittles and Twiggy seemed happy and proud, having endured the windy night at the summit of Match Patch.

Bluegrass caught up to me as I was taking a short break. When I passed him earlier, he was still in his tent. We had never camped together but had been leapfrogging with one another for the past 12 days. He explained to me that he had given up his apartment, sold his car, and had saved up enough money to hike long-distance trails for the next four years. He was on a strict budget, so he was planning to camp at Deer Park Mountain Shelter, which was three miles before Hot Springs. The next day he would hike into Hot Springs, enjoy some town food, resupply, and then hike five miles north to a campsite for the night. This way he avoided the cost of lodging in Hot Springs.

After hiking 20 miles, I reached the side trail for the Deer Park Mountain Shelter. I was tempted to stop with Bluegrass. My blister was not bothering me anymore, so I decided to continue three more miles into Hot Springs. Unfortunately, hiking too fast for 23 miles, especially downhill, is a mistake many hikers make. My left shin was killing me as the trail led me down Hot Spring's Main Street. For lodging, I registered at the Iron Horse Station. I rested

The 360 degree views as I hiked over the ridgelines of Match Patch, were spectacular.

and iced my shin for two days but still could not walk on it without sharp pain. I had developed a stress fracture in my left shin.

I started looking at my options and realized there was only one. I knew the only cure for this type of injury would have to be weeks of avoiding the constant pounding that the AT required. I have noticed that many hikers abruptly end their hike due to an injury. I was again one of those casualties. I was devastated.

I called Penny to tell her my predicament, and she was able to make contact with our good friends Jim and Terry Patka from Anchorage. They were driving from Indianapolis to their condo in Myrtle Beach. They had just attended the NCAA basketball national championships in Indianapolis and happened to be driving through on I-40, which was very close to Hot Springs.

After they arrived, we enjoyed a great steak dinner at the Iron Horse Station. Jim wanted to hike a hundred yards up the Appalachian Trail so he could let others know that he had hiked

A pleasant visit with Bluegrass. After saving some cash and selling most of his possessions, he seemed excited to have enough money to hike long distant trails for the next four years.

on the AT. We made that happen the next morning before leaving.

After rescuing me, we drove away from Hot Springs three days after I had arrived. I was a little depressed. I had hiked a total of 21 days and had only accomplished 275 miles of the 2180 miles of the Appalachian Trail. This trail had knocked me down and had beaten me up. I felt defeated and was feeling all kinds of mixed emotions. I asked myself, "Maybe this dream is beyond my capabilities." I again realized I was not as young as I apparently thought I was. My mind would say yes, but my body would tell me no.

We arrived that evening in Myrtle Beach, and I was bedridden for the next two days. I flew out of Myrtle Beach and headed back to Anchorage on April 9, 1915. After arriving home, I continued to analyze my inability to conquer this trail. Was my competitive spirit part of the problem? Penny has frequently reminded me that my competitive spirit can sometime be a negative. Many times she has insisted that I slow down, stop and smell the roses. I was beginning to realize that successful long-distance hiking on the Appalachian Trail was for the very experienced hiker.

CHAPTER 3

Mount Katahdin Southbound

"To be tested is good. The challenged life
may be the best therapist."
—Gail Sheehy

After three months of recovering from my shin stress fracture, I decided to head back to the northernmost part of the Appalachian Trail on July 4, 2015. That meant long flights from Anchorage to Boston and long bus rides from Boston to Millinocket, Maine. The Appalachian Trail Hostel in Millinocket had a special deal that included picking a hiker up at the bus stop, a night's lodging, a hearty breakfast the next morning, and then a 20 -mile shuttle to the base of Mount Katahdin.

Since it was July, I thought it might be a little cooler starting this section hike in Northern Maine. It was a beautiful day with blue skies, but the 85-degree temperature was a little warm for this Alaskan. I found myself stopping and taking many breaks as I struggled up the steep slopes that were filled with rocks and boulders. Unfortunately, I had miscalculated how much water I needed and soon became dehydrated.

After an exhausting climb and thinking I was at the top of Mount Katahdin, I came around a corner and experienced an '*are you kidding me*' moment, as I looked up and realized there was a very difficult climb ahead.

The long rugged climb up to the 5000-foot summit was a fitting grand finale for northbound thru-hikers, having hiked 2180 miles from Springer Mountain in Georgia. I started wondering if this was a foolish way to start a section hike. I tried to conserve the little water I had left as I reached the summit. To verify my ascent, I asked a fellow hiker to take a picture of me next to the sign. The miserable swarming black flies were out in force, so I soon started my descent back down the very steep grade I had just come up.

It was a slow two-mile descent to the next water source. There, I rested and slowly drank a liter of water. After filling my water bottle again, I continued down the steep challenging slopes. Reaching the campsite at the base, I was totally exhausted and dehydrated again. It had taken me nine hours to hike the ten miles. I drank another two liters of water but was still unable to pee.

The next morning, I was relieved to find a fairly easy ten-mile trail to the Abol Bridge store. I spent an hour there, resting, having lunch, and drinking two bottles of sport drinks. I finally was able to pee a trickle for the first time in 24

It was a slow, meticulous and tiring descent down Kahtahdin.

hours and decided to take three sports drinks with me to help continue to hydrate. The Hurd Brook Shelter was only three miles ahead from Abol Bridge. As I arrived there, I found over 30 hikers tenting around the large camping area.

After a good night's sleep, I left at daybreak. Soon after leaving, it started pouring. The rain felt refreshing, but the humidity was very high. After hiking five miles in the downpour, I realized I was not wearing my glasses. To go back and try to find them along the trail would be like trying to find a needle in a haystack. I continued on.

After a couple of hours, the rain finally stopped, but the heat and humidity was weakening me. I was losing too much body liquid through my sweat, and was unable to replenish it all, with enough water. I had to take an hour break every three miles. In addition, the trail was muddy from the downpour, and without my glasses, everything became a blur. I tripped and fell hard, two different times that day. It was a difficult 12-mile struggle getting to the Rainbow Stream Shelter. There were several hikers tenting on a knoll behind the shelter. It was a nice large tenting area, so I found a level spot and set up my tent. I cooked a beef dinner, but could only force down a third of it.

I left at six the next morning, hoping for cooler temperatures. By 7:00 a.m., the temperature was 90 and rising. I was suffering. I continued taking hour-long water breaks every few miles. The tripping and hard falls continued for the next two days. It took me 12 hours of hiking to complete 16 miles each of those days.

To start my sixth day, both hiking poles were beyond repair and my eyesight was blurry. I left the Cooper Brooks Falls Shelter with very sore ribs and with some kind of internal bleeding. I had been taking a lot of ibuprofen for my aching rib cage, and, this, along with my dehydration problems, was probably causing the black stools.

Three miles later, just past Crawford Pond, I stumbled out of the woods onto the narrow gravel Kokadjo-Pond Road. Three cars were parked there. Come to find out, it was Scott Jurek and his support crew. He was averaging 47 miles a day, trying to beat the AT speed record. They had tented there and were getting ready to leave.

After Scott left jogging northbound, I let his crew know my serious condition and told them I was afraid I would die on the AT if I continued through 50 more miles of this remote 100 Mile Wilderness. They took one look at me and knew I was in bad shape. They were more than willing to give me a ride out of this very remote place.

They drove me ten miles to a paved road where I was able to hitch a 20 -mile ride back to Millinocket. After washing my sweaty clothes at a Laundromat, I hitched a 60 -mile ride back to Bangor, Maine. Near the bus station, I eagerly consumed a couple of hamburgers and two large milkshakes. That evening, I was able to get a bus back to Boston airport and eventually flights back to Anchorage.

After living in Alaska for the past 50 years, I found that my body does not acclimate well, hiking up mountains in temperatures of 80 and above. I was fortunate to find Scott Jurek's support crew camped on this very remote logging road. I think I was being looked after from above. Unfortunately, this was the third time in five months that injuries on the AT were sending me home. I was discouraged, but these setbacks were somehow making me more determined. My competitive spirit was motivating this, sort of, revenge factor within me. Deep inside, I knew this challenging trail was not going to defeat me. In boxing terms, I would eventually be back for round four.

CHAPTER 4

More Tennessee and North Carolina

"The Mountains are calling and I must go"
—John Muir

It took six months for my ribs to heal. I hated not finishing something I had set out to accomplish. I had stayed in shape over the winter and was ready to go back and do better. It had been over 12 months since I first started hiking the AT, so my status had changed from being a revered thru-hiker to a LASHER, known on the AT as a "Long Ass Section Hiker."

I had purchased a much lighter backpack, tent, and sleeping bag, which, all three combined, weighed a total of five pounds. I had also decided to go without a stove. That meant no fuel to carry. I did have a quart titanium teakettle that I could boil water over a campfire. I was carrying dehydrated dinners that you can pour boiling water right into the dinner's lightweight container. When the backpack was fully loaded with all my gear, including food and water for a few days, the total weight was 20 pounds, half the weight of my original pack the previous year.

I was determined to be more careful and hike some serious miles this time around. Penny was now getting used to dropping me off at the airport and seeing me returning home after several days. My past success rate spoke for itself. This time she kissed me and simply said, "See you in a couple of weeks."

I left Anchorage on March 4, 2016, heading for Hot Springs, North Carolina. This is where I had exited the trail ten months earlier due to a shin stress fracture. Most hikers the first of March would now be leaving Georgia, 275 miles behind me. This meant heading north from Hot Springs, the shelters and campsites would be a lot less crowded.

Many of my friends had voiced, "You're crazy." This was actually making me question my sanity. I told myself, "I love the outdoors, and I love a challenge." I started remembering the spectacular views after climbing and hiking the ridgelines. I reminded myself of the calming effect of hiking along a quiet lake or the sound of hiking or camping next to a cascading stream. The flowers, the trees, the sound of birds in the morning, and the peacefulness of hiking through the woods were all calling me back. I would have to endure some very difficult days, but that was part of the challenge of long-distance hiking. Now that I had justified my insanity, I was bound for Hot Springs.

After eight hours on planes, I took the commuter train to downtown Atlanta to the Greyhound Bus Station. I was a little frustrated when I found out that I had to go all the way to Knoxville, Tennessee, to get a bus to Ashville, North Carolina. The crowds at the Atlanta and Knoxville Greyhound stations were a little scary. I was not used to bus stations in a large city, especially in the middle of the night. Many were not passengers but some type of night people finding the warmth of the terminal. As the night wore on, passengers would line up as their destination was called. After watching two buses depart, Knoxville was finally called. I sat in the front of the bus where I felt a little safer.

Arriving in Knoxville, Tennessee, it was about a 30-minute wait for my bus departure to Ashville. After a sleepless night, the bus finally arrived at the Ashville Greyhound Station at 9:30 a.m. I was planning to hitch the remaining 30 miles. I hiked two miles to Route 25. Once there, I held up my sign for Hot Springs.

A thousand cars had zoomed by when finally a car honked and pulled over. James was his name, and he was a former thru-hiker who lived in Ashville. I asked him how far he was going, and he said, "I'm taking you the whole way to Hot Springs." My first trail magic, and I hadn't even started hiking yet. He went over 60 miles out of his way for this very impressive gesture. I bought him lunch in Hot Springs, and he shared some good hiking advice from his AT thru-hike from the previous year.

Hot Springs is the first town through which the AT goes directly down Main Street. Usually hikers will take a zero day there to rest, do laundry, fuel up, and resupply. There are many housing options in Hot Springs. I was very tired from the all-night travel and decided to stay at Elmer's. He offers spacious rooms to hikers right on Main Street.

I must have really blacked out because I did not wake until ten the next morning. I stopped at the hikers outfitter store before leaving town to make sure I had enough food. I was planning a five-day hike to cover the 62 miles to Uncle Johnny's Hostel in Erwin. The outfitter store on Main Street in Hot Springs is very well stocked, and every hiker on the AT makes a resupply stop there.

At noon I started hiking and enjoyed a relaxing climb out of Hot Springs on a beautiful day. I took my time and hiked 11 miles up to Spring Mountain Shelter, located just above 3500 feet. It was a nice trail, and I was feeling great to be back.

There was a family of four tenting nearby; they had a nice campfire going. I pitched my tent about 70 feet from them and, after getting settled, asked if I could boil some water over their fire for my dehydrated chicken dinner. They encouraged me to do so. They were on a two-day hiking trip, and we enjoyed each other's company. My aging body was tired, and I turned in about 9:00 p.m. and slept well.

The next day I was up at daybreak, and the family of four already had a campfire going. I broke camp, said my good-byes, and started hiking at 7:00 a.m. Ten miles into the hike, I summited Camp Creek Bald above 4500 feet. Five more miles into the hike, I arrived at Jerry Cabin Shelter at mile 300. There were several hikers there. I set up my tent and visited with two hikers who were staying in the shelter. I started a campfire, boiled water, and ate a delicious hot beef-stew dinner.

I feel there are three main factors that determine how far a hiker usually travels each day. The first is a hiker's physical condition. A well-conditioned hiker usually hikes at a faster pace. The second factor is how many hours a hiker wants to spend on the trail each day. The third main factor is how heavy one's backpack is.

I stopped and visited with a couple of young guys camping along the trail that day. They were having a great time averaging five miles a day. Their packs weighed 50 pounds each. They were even packing camp chairs. A heavier load slows a hiker down, especially going up those mountains.

I constantly reminded myself to take it easy for the first couple of weeks. I did not need another injury that would send me home early. Some hikers average 5 to 8 miles a day, some average 18 or more miles a day, and most AT hikers average something in-between. Many hikers will take advantage of the free shakedowns that are available at most hiker outfitter stores. A shakedown is when an experienced hiker or employee goes through a hiker's pack and tells them what they do not need. Some hikers end up sending 10 or more pounds home on the spot.

The next morning, with blue skies above, I left Jerry Cabin Shelter at sunrise for a 16-mile hike to Hogback Ridge Shelter.

There was a long climb up Frozen Knob at 4500 feet, but the trail was smooth. I was the only hiker there, so I decided to stay in the shelter. A big white mouse kept me awake most of the night. When it would make some noise in the rafters, I would turn my headlamp on and point the light toward the scratching. This would make the mouse disappear into the top of the wall. This went on all night. Mice are often a nuisance at the shelters. Some are bolder than others. Believe it or not, hikers eventually get used to them.

I left this shelter at daybreak. Near the end of the hike, I became a little dehydrated as I slowly struggled up Big Bald Mountain. Halfway up, I came to a nice mountain stream where I stopped for a long break, quenching my thirst. Several day hikers passed by me, as Big Bald was a popular mountain for locals to climb. Finally reaching the summit at 5500 feet, there were spectacular 360-degree views. Most of the Appalachian Trail is in the woods without many views. When I did get a view at the top of a mountain, I was usually very tired and was ready for a long enjoyable break.

I hiked another mile into the woods to a very roomy and clean Big Bald Shelter at 5300 feet. There was a nice stream of spring water nearby. I found a lot of dead branches around the camping area, so I decided to start a campfire. A section hiker arrived, and we chatted until it got dark, when we finally dozed off.

I forgot how steep some of these climbs were. On a daily basis, the AT had a way of letting this hiker know his age. I departed Big Bald Shelter in awe of a beautiful sunrise. It would be a 16-mile hike into Erwin, Georgia. I would be descending from 5000 to 2000 feet on the hike. In the process, however, there were 20 steep little hills that would total about 3000 feet of climbing. Hiking on a ridgeline as I neared the end of the hike, there were spectacular views looking far below at the Nolichucky River Valley. The descent off this ridge into Erwin had over 20 switchbacks.

I checked in at Uncle Johnny's Hostel in Erwin (mile 342). Waiting for me at the hostel was a two-pound box of trail mix that my wife had mailed from home. I took a needed shower, then got a ride to a great little hamburger and ice-cream shop down the street. I devoured a giant cheeseburger with lettuce-tomato-onions and bacon and a very thick milkshake made with real pineapples. I had been dreaming about town food all day. Town food tastes so good after strenuous hiking all day.

Uncle Johnny's is located on the trail as you come out of the woods. The hostel has several private rooms and a large bunk room, all for reasonable prices. Besides a laundry facility and bathhouse, they have a well-stocked resupply store. I briefly met a thru-hiker named Crash, who was being shuttled up the trail 23 miles the next morning heading northbound. I figured I would never see him again.

I departed Erwin at 10:30 a.m. on March 11, after a hearty breakfast of ham, eggs, toast, and plenty of coffee. Uncle Johnny's Hostel offers a couple of free rides to restaurants, which is included in the price for a night's lodging. After departing, a thru-hiker named Jones passed me. We visited a bit and then he was on his way.

It was an exhausting 12-mile hike up 3000 feet to the base of Unaka Mountain. I camped with Justin and his dog, Pancho. He was on a two-day hike and was planning to climb Unaka the next morning. After setting up our tents, we visited, cooked, and enjoyed one another's company next to a warming campfire. After nightfall, we climbed into our tents for the night.

I said good-bye to Justin and departed camp at 8:00 a.m. A half mile down the trail, I passed Jones who had pitched his tent at a campsite next to some piped spring water. Jones was eating breakfast and was relaxing around a campfire before breaking camp. I visited for a few minutes as I filled my water bottles for the steep hike ahead.

When I arrived, Justin had a campfire going and invited me to stay. After hiking alone all day, I did not hesitate to set up my tent and enjoy trail talk around the comfort of a campfire.

The summit of Unaka is over 5000 feet. During the climb up, I started to create a poem about AT hikers. As the phrases slowly fit in place, it turned a difficult climb into an easy climb. I was at the top before I knew it. A perfect example of mind over matter. The miles really did go by quicker when I found myself in deep thought.

Hikers in the woods, They don't mind the pain.
Hikers in the woods, Are they really sane?
Climbing up the mountains, With their worn tired feet.
Moving very steady, With a rhythmic beat.
Hikers in the woods, They don't mind the weather.
The journey is what brings them joy.
Miles and miles bring many smiles.
Hikers in the woods.

The day was cloudy during the 14-mile hike to the Clyde Smith Shelter. At the shelter were two brothers, Cameron and Dayton, on a spring-break hike, and three section hikers from Brooksville, Florida. After cooking and visiting for a while, I retired to the sleeping bag at camper midnight (Sundown), which was then about 8:00 p.m.

As I left Clyde Smith Shelter at daybreak, it started raining. My goal was to get over the 6000-foot summit of Rohn Mountain. Rohn Mountain is one of the highest mountains on the AT. As I climbed, the wind started howling. The gusts were exceeding at least 40 miles an hour. It was more than a little scary, with trees everywhere threatening to come down at any moment. It was a long two-hour climb.

At the summit, I met another hiker named Backtrack going southbound. He did the entire Appalachian Trail the year before and was doing a long southbound section hike to Gatlinburg, which was back in the Smoky Mountain National Park. He advised me of more enormous winds a couple of miles ahead at Carver's Gap. We were both wet and chilled, so we were soon on our way.

When I reached Carver's Gap, I realized Backtrack had not exaggerated. There was a wind tunnel blowing at least 50 mph. It lasted for two miles over Jane Bald and beyond. I hiked in rain, thick fog, and very cold winds all day. It was a very challenging 16-mile hike. When I arrived at Over the Mountain Shelter, Peach, a southbound thru-hiker, arrived at the very same time from the north. Peach had encountered the same intense wet, windy, and frigid weather for 18 miles from Mountaineer Shelter.

As we walked toward this very unique shelter (a barn turned into a shelter), the fog lifted, blue sky appeared, and we more than welcomed the warm sun. Also appearing was "Moonpie," a gal who helps maintain this part of the trail. She had soda pop and chocolate moonpies. Peach and I were in hog heaven about the turn of events. What a difference 30 minutes can make. Moonpie visited with us for an hour, and we graciously thanked her for her generosity.

Peach was from Dallas, Texas, and we somehow got a campfire going with damp wood and talked nonstop for several hours. He told me about the trail I was about to venture out on, and I did the same for him. As we ate and snacked, it was obvious we were also quite hungry for conversation. We hung our gear on mouse-proof string with hooks, which are at most shelters. We slept well after an exhausting day of hiking.

The next morning, Peach and I were up at daybreak visiting again. After morning chores and breaking camp, we hiked out the 200 yards to the trail together. We shook hands having shared one another's company for the past 14 hours. It was as if we had become best friends. Peach would be leaving the empty shelters from the north and be heading into the masses hiking northward. We wished the best to one another and then he departed southbound and I northbound, never to see one another again.

I only had a ten miler planned for the day and was anxious to get to Mountain Harbour Hostel and relax for a while. I had been dreaming of a Subway sandwich and found myself obsessed with quenching my thirst with some chocolate milk.

There was not a cloud in the sky. The day was warm with a slight breeze, so I decided to really slow down and take it all in. Robins and many other birds were singing all morning. They seemed happy as well that the storm from the day before was over.

The climb up Hump Mountain took me up to 5500 feet. The 360-degree view was breathtaking. The bald at the top went on for a very relaxing three miles. It was nice to be out of the woods for a while. What a contrast from the day before.

Eventually I entered the woods again and descended 3000 feet, arriving at the hostel about 1:00 p.m. Shannon was the owner of the hostel, which is less than a half mile from the trail. I took a shower, did laundry, and hitched a ride to Subway.

A couple of guys on a two-week section hike arrived around 7:00 p.m. One of the hikers told me that the night before he woke up at 3:00 a.m. in the Stan Murray Shelter. On his chest stood a mouse staring him in the face. He instinctively hollered and jumped out of his hammock, sending the mouse flying through the air. Both hikers decided to move outside where they found trees to tie their hammocks to. They were able to eventually go back to sleep but still seemed a little shook from the experience.

I slept in and left the hostel at 11:00 a.m. the next day. Five and a half miles into my hike, I saw a sign for water. The day was warm, and after a 1000-foot climb, I was thirsty. I turned and followed the blue blazes a very short distance to a nice ice-cold spring. Many times, Blue-Blazed Trails will take a hiker to a water source or a parking lot trailhead. Sometimes a Blue-Blazed Trail provides a hiker a shortcut avoiding a difficult White-Blaze section. Other times the blue blazes may lead a hiker over an old section of the AT.

I drank about a pint of ice-cold spring water through my filter and filled my bottle again to take with me. Just as I turned and started back toward the trail, two retired couples were walking toward me. They said, "Aren't you going a little farther to see the waterfalls? It's only around the corner." I was in a hurry again, so I said, "No, thanks," and continued toward the white blazes.

Back on the trail, I went about 100 yards and very clearly heard my wife's voice insisting that I slow down and enjoy the hike. It brought me to a screeching halt. I did an about-face and went back to Jones Falls and had a most cooling and enjoyable half-hour break with eight day hikers.

These day hikers had hiked for hours just to get up here, and I was only 50 feet away from the beautiful falls. I had a pleasant conversation with Kim. She and her husband had lived and worked in Louisiana all their lives. When they retired, they said to themselves, "Let's move to the mountains." Now they have become day hikers with unlimited choices for their hikes and loving their new lifestyle. The millions of people who live near the Appalachian Trail are blessed with all the many different trails and mountains to climb. They also have the luxury of carrying ultra light packs and waiting for nice weather to do their day or weekend hikes.

After a 14-mile hike, I set up my tent next to a loud cascading stream with two hikers named Coach and Boomerang. The sound of it was soothing. I slept sound all night. After a breakfast bar, I departed before daybreak. Coach and Boomerang were already gone, and I had not heard them leave. I moved along nicely through the North Carolina woods for the first ten miles until I hit Laurel Falls Park. The park started with a beautiful groomed trail. Soon I came to hundreds of huge stone steps that led me down to the waterfalls. What a beautiful park and waterfalls. I was in awe of it all. The park was a welcome little adventure from walking in the woods. At the bottom of the gorge, the AT continued alongside the fast moving stream.

My first trail encounter with Crash as he explained how slack packing works.

Just past the Falls, I ran into Crash heading southbound. He was doing another slack pack carrying a 5-pound pack, and I was getting ready for another climb with my 20-pound pack. I was thinking, maybe I should get smart and start doing some slack packing. It would definitely help make this mountain hiking a little more enjoyable.

I briefly ran into Crash 70 miles back in Erwin at Uncle Johnny's. When he slack-packs, he hires a driver to take him 20-plus miles north into the mountains and then hikes back south (usually downhill) to the same hostel he stayed at the night before. Many hostels promote this because it means you will stay at their hostel for two nights. The next day, the shuttle driver takes him back north where they had dropped him off the day before and then he continues his march northbound. Crash and I visited for about five minutes, and I told him if we met up again, I was interested in doing a "slack pack" or two with him. He said he would like that.

When I eventually made it to Route 321, I hitched a ride two miles into Hampton to stay at the Braemar Castle Hostel. After registering, I took a long hot shower. Afterward, I hiked down the street and enjoyed a fantastic prime rib sandwich at a food stand. I then resupplied at Brown's store. Dutton Brown, owner of the hostel, also owns the grocery store. The hostel was clean, very spacious, had many private rooms, all for a very reasonable price.

The next morning, Dutton drove me back to the trail at daybreak. I was planning a three-day push to Damascus. Climbing nine miles up to Vandeventer Shelter, I gained more than 2000 feet. The trail then became kind. At the shelter, I saw that Crash had written in the shelter log. All shelters have a notebook log that hikers are encouraged to sign. This lets other hikers know that they have passed through. It also helps search-and-rescue teams to locate a missing hiker. Crash was about two hours ahead of me, and he wrote that he was planning to stay at the Double Spring Shelter for the night. It was noon, and after already hiking nine tough miles, I wasn't sure if I could hike 14 more miles to catch up to him.

The trail started following this ridgeline, straight north. The previous 350 miles, the AT would curve around mountains heading east, west, south, and eventually north, making me wonder if little progress was being made, moving toward Maine. As I hiked along this welcomed smooth trail, I could look down on either side of this very high ridge and see lush valleys of green pastures, lakes, and towns. It was sort of like flying slow motion in a small plane, looking down at the terrain below. The trail going reasonably straight gave me a feeling that I was making good time going north.

I arrived at the Iron Mountain Shelter at 4:00 p.m., with seven miles to go. After a short break, I felt good and decided to hike on. I finally arrived at Double Spring Shelter just before dusk. Crash, Seeker, and Adam had a large pile of wood gathered for a campfire. We hung out, and all enjoyed one another's company until 10:30 p.m. Crash informed me that this 40-mile stretch that we were on is known as the Tennessee Turnpike.

Hiking long distances brings much joy and, at the same time, can be extremely demanding. The trail will reveal a person's resolve, their mental toughness, and their true colors. Many times the experiences on the trail provide an opportunity for a hiker to reflect not only on one's character but also on one's life. It can be a time of much soul searching. The experience of hiking a long-distance hike gives one an incredible feeling of accomplishment, but also may reveal a different direction a hiker should follow in life. Seeker's purpose in hiking the AT was to help him find out what God's will was for the rest of his life. To quote Ivy Baker Pries: "The world is round and the place which may seem like the end may also be the beginning."

Crash woke up the next morning at six and enthusiastically shouted, "It's hiker time." The temperature was a chilly 40 degrees as I slowly crawled out of my bag. I meticulously started my routine of carefully putting on my toe sock liners, massaging my feet a bit and then putting on the outer socks. I pulled my insoles out of my sleeping bag where they had been drying out overnight and slipped them into my hiking shoes.

After slipping my shoes on, I retrieved my food bag from where it was hung from a tree branch. The morning routine continued as I stuffed the sleeping bag in its container and placed it and all the rest of my gear into the backpack in the same order as I did every morning. I always had my snacks and water prepared the night before for the next day's hike. It was all a ritual that was now taking me about 45 minutes. Seeker was all snuggled up with only his eyes peeking out of his sleeping bag, watching with interest as Crash and I went through our morning chores.

Crash and I left the shelter with our headlamps on at 6:45 a.m. Four miles into the hike, we took a snack break at a shelter where there was a picnic table and some ice-cold spring water coming out of a pipe. It was cloudy, but the trail was smooth. Eight miles into the hike, we stopped for another short snack break. This experience of hiking with someone was new for me, and I liked hiking with Crash. My first 450 miles of the AT I had been hiking virtually solo. I had hiked the last 12 days in a row and that was one of the reasons I had been able to catch up to him. Crash was in his mid-60s and from New Hampshire. He was a former thru-hiker and, over the years, has done many section hikes of the AT. He had a wealth of information about the Appalachian Trail.

The last six miles into Damascus was a gradual 2000-foot descent. About four miles before arriving, we crossed into the state of Virginia. The 20-mile hike was easier and more enjoyable than the norm. Arriving in Damascus and the state of Virginia was definitely another milestone reached.

CHAPTER 5

Southern Virginia

"When I first open my eyes upon the morning meadows and look out upon the beautiful world, I thank God I am alive."
—Ralph Waldo Emerson

Damascus is the second town on the AT where the white blazes lead a hiker right down the Main Street. There are lots of lodging available. It is known as the friendliest town on the Appalachian Trail. The Creeper Trail is a big deal there as well. The 17-mile bike trail follows a nicely groomed old railroad bed along a beautiful cascading stream. Many van companies haul bikers up into the mountains, and a biker can coast all the way back along this trail into Damascus. The AT follows some of the Creeper Trail.

Crash decided during our rest day that it was time for my first slack pack. Woodchuck from Woodchuck Hostel drove us up north into the mountains to mile 493. We found Jones there breaking down his tent, getting ready to continue north. We were slack packing 23 miles back to Damascus. I had been leapfrogging with Jones for the past 150 miles. We visited for a while and eventually wished each other safe hiking.

The temperature was chilly, and there was frost everywhere. For that reason, our pace was brisk. Our first ascent went up to Buzzard Rock.

I was feeling good on a frosty morning as I hiked toward Buzzard Rock at 5000 feet.

After nine miles of gradual descent, we stopped at Lost Mountain Shelter and ate our Subway sandwiches that we had bought the night before. Another goal for the day was to reach Mojo's restaurant before it closed at 5:00 p.m. We continued hiking through the woods and eventually hit the Creeper Trail.

The ten-mile trek on this Creeper Trail crossed 20 bridges, some of them quite long over the cascading stream. Arriving back in Damascus, we had accomplished our goals for the day, including arriving at Mojo's in time for an enjoyable meal.

Living in Anchorage, a city of approximately 250,000 people, I am always careful about avoiding traffic when crossing streets.

Hiking in the woods ten hours a day, I never had to worry about speeding vehicles. When I came to a town every three or four days, I found myself conditioned to not paying attention to traffic. I came close to being run over two different times in Damascus. Crash told me I had better be more careful or I might have to be sent home in a casket.

The people in Damascus seem genuinely friendly. A couple was sitting on their porch as I went by with my backpack, and invited me in for a piece of their homemade chocolate pie. Another man asked where I was from, and when I told him Anchorage, he wanted to know all about the Iditarod Sled Dog Race. The excellent cook and owner of Mojo's came up to our table and just started chatting.

People seem to be upbeat, proud of their little town and will go out of their way to make a hiker feel welcome. Crash and I stayed at the Hiker's Inn, a very nice home/hostel, owned and operated by Paul and Lee, a very friendly husband-and-wife team. Woodchuck Hostel was also known to be hiker friendly, located just as a hiker first comes into town.

On a Tuesday morning at 8:00 a.m., Woodchuck delivered us back up to mile 493 to continue our trek northbound. The ground was frozen as Crash and I started our climb up Mount Rodgers, Virginia's highest peak. It was chilly, and we had to keep moving to stay warm. A few hours later, we made our way down through the Grayson Highlands. We were pleased as the temperature warmed up into the 40s. We spotted about 25 wild ponies in four different places over the next few miles. They were not spooky at all and would not even look up from munching on grass as we hiked right by them. It was the highlight of the day.

I experienced an incredible high, hiking by the wild ponies of the Grayson Highlands.

We arrived at Hurricane Mountain Shelter at 5:00 p.m. after a long but enjoyable 19-mile hike. We found Tenderfoot there. Crash had camped with him a few nights back in the Smoky Mountains. Tenderfoot was a thru-hiker on a strict budget. When he needed a zero day, he would usually take the rest day at a shelter to avoid the extra expense of a motel room. He hiked the AT in a very thrifty manner.

The next day the three of us departed Hurricane Shelter at daybreak with the intent of making 18 miles to the Partnership Shelter. This campsite was located right next to the Mt. Rodgers Visitor Center. Outside the visitor center, there was a local phone where hikers could call and have pizza delivered. Crash and I each ordered a large super supreme and a quart of soda pop. Pizza never tasted so good. We each shared our pizza with Tenderfoot. His food mostly consisted of Top Ramen and other cheap dehydrated food he would buy at some big box store.

Around 7:00 p.m., a thru-hiker named Goat came hiking in. He always tented, got up every morning at four, and was averaging an insane 35 miles a day. As he sat at the picnic table in front of the shelter, eating his dinner, he shared many hilarious experiences from his hiking. For icing on the cake, Boomerang showed up with half a gallon of ice cream and a large bag of homemade oatmeal cookies from his girlfriend, who lived nearby. I had not seen Boomerang for over 100 miles, but we owed him big time after his welcome treat. We all quickly found our spoons, and the trail magic disappeared in a few minutes under a full moon. It was an enjoyable night at the camp.

Crash and I left the Partnership Shelter at daybreak for a ten-mile hike to the rundown Relax Inn. Heavy rain was in the forecast, so Crash and I decided to shorten our hike and share a room there. Our bodies were demanding calories, so before showering, we hurried up the road 200 yards to the Barn Restaurant and enjoyed steak sandwiches, french fries, and milkshakes.

We rested all afternoon. That evening, we walked up the road to a convenient store at a gas station to resupply. There was also a Mexican restaurant, so we sat down and fueled up even more for the next day's hike. We obviously had developed the hiker's appetite from hiking so many miles each day.

It rained all night. By 8:00 a.m. it had not let up, so I packed up, put my rain gear on, and started hiking. Crash said he was going to wait for the rain to stop. Actually, he told me later, that he had hiked up to the Barn Restaurant for breakfast. If I would have known breakfast was in the cards, I might have thought twice about hiking in the rain..

At 10:00 a.m., I stopped at a shelter and took a 20-minute break out of the rain. About ten miles into the hike, Crash had caught up to me at the first quarter mark of the AT. That meant we had finished the first 545 miles of the Appalachian Trail. It was an emotional lift as we took pictures of each other at this significant milestone. This little sign, a town day, a slack pack, some trail magic, and finding a hiking companion, all helped to keep me mentally positive. After a few hundred miles, hiking hour after hour, day after day, maintaining a mental challenge on the AT, sometimes is as difficult as the physical challenge. After a 14-mile hike, we ended up at Knot Maul Branch Shelter. I started a campfire, boiled water and mixed up some Gatorade for the next day's hike.

Crash and I hardly ever hiked together but always planned to end up at the same place at the end of the day. We both liked to start hiking at daybreak, were avid golfers, had raced sled dogs for ten years, and seemed to enjoy one another's company.

I am often the first hiker out of camp in the morning. That means I ran into many fine single threads that spiders somehow string across the trail during the night. Usually these threads would hit me in the face every half mile or so. It amazes me how these spiders can spread this single thread six to eight feet across the trail during the night. One day there was a leaf dangling in one of those threads in the middle of the trail. Instinctively I lifted my phone and captured a unique video of this leaf suspended and floating in the air.

At daybreak the next day, I left Knot Maul Branch Shelter with my headlamp on, knowing that the 20-mile hike we planned that day included three tough climbs. Crash usually would leave about 20 minutes after me. Tenderfoot occasionally camped with us and always left about an hour after us. His pack weighed about 40 pounds, but he moved effortlessly. He was 26 years old, was strong as an ox, hiked in crocs, and around midday would zoom past us.

The highlight of the hike was taking a 30-minute lunch break after climbing a fairly steep 2100-foot climb to the summit of Chestnut Knob. Crash had just caught up with me as we reached the summit of this bald, nine miles into our hike. After taking our backpacks off, we sat down on some dry grass that overlooked some lush farmland far below that seemed to stretch for miles. I found out later that many of these farms were owned and worked by Amish families. They have been known to serve hikers a meal. They meet hikers up the trail a ways at a road crossing and take them to their farm by horse and wagon.

Animal and Tenderfoot caught up to us as we were picnicking. We all eventually continued over some challenging terrain and arrived at Jenkins Shelter at 5:00 p.m. We all claimed a spot on the floor of the shelter and neatly lined our mats and sleeping bags alongside one another.

Just before dark, we were joined by a heavyset hiker and her dog. There was maybe two feet of space between Animal and me. Instead of setting up her tent, like most any hiker does when the weather is nice and a shelter is filled, she started pushing all her gear into this tiny space between Animal and me.

Once she had wedged between us, she climbed into her sleeping bag and called her dog to jump up into the shelter right next to me. The dog smelled like ten rats that had been dead for a month. Even though I am not, I automatically shouted, "I'm allergic to dogs." She sadly answered, "You mean I can't let my dog sleep with all of us tonight?" She finally realized how bad her dog smelled and took the dog down to the stream and then washed him in the water we used to drink from. She eventually tied him up to a tree about 30 feet from the shelter, where he remained content the rest of the night. As soon as this gal laid her head down, she started snoring. I mean this snore was the loudest I have ever heard, and unfortunately, it went on all night. I could not sleep with this loud snoring a couple of feet away from my ears.

With little sleep the night before, the first climb out of camp was exhausting. Crash easily caught me before I reached the top. Once on the ridgeline, the trail became kind, and our pace increased. We arrived in Bland, Virginia, at mile 588 at noon. There was a cell-phone tower next to the trail, and I was happy to make contact with my wife to find out all was well at home.

Rain was in the forecast, so we called Bubba, a shuttle driver from Bland, for a three-mile ride to the motel in town. We enjoyed ice-cream treats at the Dairy Queen, a great sandwich at Subway, and resupplied at the Dollar Store down the street. Our appetites easily convinced us to order pizza delivery that evening. It rained all night.

Crash called Bubba at 9:00 a.m. to shuttle us back to the trail. He climbs hills much faster than me, but our pace is about the same going downhill or on even surfaces. The trail started with another steep climb, and he went way ahead of me from the get-go.

At the top of the ridge, the trail became smooth, but the wind was howling. It continued with gusts up to around 40 mph for most of the day. There was a one-mile stretch that went down and out of the wind. I stopped there behind a large boulder and ate my lunch. Back up on the ridge, the wind continued to blow, but the view looking down on either side of the ridge featured more lush green farmland.

There are many trails that cross the AT. As I hiked mile after mile through the woods, I found myself daydreaming a lot. I spent a lot of time revisiting people and past events. When I would snap out of my thoughts, I would quickly start looking for a white blaze. When they wouldn't appear, a little panic would set in; I would wonder if I took the wrong trail. When a white blaze would finally show itself, there would be a huge breath of relief. It happens every day.

I arrived at Trent Grocery, a small convenience store where Crash and I had agreed to meet. The grocery had a fast-food portion that served breakfast, lunch, and dinner.

The place sat alone in the countryside. It had one gas pump and was busy with the locals constantly coming and going. The customers seemed to know everyone else, and the southern accent and jiving that took place was very entertaining, especially for this northern boy. We found out that Trent Grocery had one

I was experiencing tranquility, scenting pine as I hiked through pine forests.

small building they rent out for $45. It had two beds, a bathroom with a shower, and a washer and dryer. We jumped on that bargain before any other hiker had a chance. The hot shower is always fantastic after a long hike, and we also were able to wash all our clothes. A mattress was so much more comfortable than sleeping on the floors of shelters.

On Monday, March 28, we left Trent Grocery at 7:30 a.m. The first eight miles was a beautiful trail through miles of rhododendron tunnels. There was another long stretch through a tall pine forest. The path was unusually flat with a brook running alongside the trail.

Nine miles into the hike, we climbed 1500 feet up Sugar Run Mountain. I wondered how it got its name. Five more miles, we arrived at the Woods Hole Hostel. The hostel is one of the best on the Appalachian Trail. Owners Michael and Neville have cows, pigs, goats, a nice bathhouse, a large bunkhouse, and a few very nice private rooms for hikers. They own 80 acres and have worked very hard over the past several years to create a very special place in the mountains for hikers. They grow all kinds of organic vegetables and offer bountiful healthy meals. They offer one-hour massages as well. Crash and I did not hesitate to have our weary bodies worked over by these experienced professionals. We thoroughly enjoyed this heavenly experience. Hikers who skip this refuge in the woods will miss one of the highlights of the AT.

The owners of the very unique Woods Hole Hostel, were very welcoming and provided a very relaxing and delightful stay.

Crash and I left the hostel the next morning refreshed and full. Neville had made us a delicious breakfast of oatmeal, toast, some fruit, and coffee. The first eight miles to Pearisburg was a fairly easy hike along a high ridgeline that offered some incredible views of the valley below. The last two miles, however, was a steep 1800-foot drop, which was slow going for two old guys. After coming out of the woods, we found ourselves in Pearisburg, Virginia. I walked to the post office to pick up a box of trail mix that Penny had sent. We then went down the street and spent an hour chowing down at an excellent Mexican restaurant.

Rather than stay at the rundown hotel in Pearisburg, Crash knew of a place three miles away in the small town of Narrows that was much better. We called Allen, who owns the MacArthur Inn. He came and picked us up shortly after. Allen was quite a character, an excellent historian, and he knew how to entertain hikers.

CHAPTER 6

Middle Virginia

"The clearest way into the Universe is
through a forest wilderness."
—John Muir

The next morning, Allen shuttled us up into the mountains for a 20-mile slack pack back to his hotel. We started hiking up along a fast-moving mountain stream. It provided a pleasant sound and was a wonderful way to start our climb.

Once we reached the top of the ridgeline, the wind was so strong that trees could have easily crashed down on us at any point. Our light packs allowed us to move swiftly under cloudy skies. We covered the 20-mile hike in seven hours.

Crash and I were entertained at the MacArthur Inn that night to their live "Ho Down" extravaganza. Over 15 very talented local musicians sat in chairs in a large circle, jamming and playing good old bluegrass music for over two hours. It was the real deal.

The next day, Allen shuttled us up to where he dropped us off the day before, and we again started hiking northbound. Many days I trip over roots and rocks that are hidden under leaves. I have fallen many times, but on this particular day, I saw stars at the end of a backward fall as my head smacked against a large rock. I got up, took my pack off, and felt for blood. Everything seemed to be OK.

I estimated that Crash was about a mile in front of me. It could have been worse. It shook me up a bit. I found a place to sit and took a break right there. There are places on the trail that are downright dangerous. That day's 13-mile hike was difficult, challenging, and mentally exhausting. Crash informed me that there was a sports store ahead and suggested I should possibly get fitted for a hockey helmet. We eventually arrived at War Spur Shelter for the night.

Leaving War Spur Shelter at daybreak, the goal was to hike 18 miles to the Niday Shelter. Crash was still packing up as I left. After a few miles along another ridgeline, I soon found myself heading down across a mile of lush green farmland. It was a welcome change from the woods. Crash eventually caught up to me, and we enjoyed a lunch break as we looked back over the two-mile valley that we had just passed through.

Back into the trees again, we trudged up this very steep climb to another ridgeline of boulders. The trail designers for the AT always seem to choose the most difficult route. It is frustrating at times, knowing there is an easier smoother route nearby. Hiking over tough terrain, we are supposed to experience a greater feeling of accomplishment, but after weeks and months, it wears on you. Many hikers, at times, have some choice words for the trail designers. We arrived at Niday Shelter at 4:00 p.m.

The next morning, again I left first out of the shelter, and the hike started with a very steep climb up to the summit of Brush Mountain. Crash caught me at the top, and we hiked a few miles together to Pickle Branch Shelter. We stopped there and took a short lunch break. Crash took off ahead of me as we climbed to a ridge of boulders called the Dragon's Back. It was slow and exhausting for this 71-year-old.

Crash, on the other hand, loved the challenges that the AT abundantly provides. He seemed to always pick up his pace as the terrain became more difficult. I estimated that Crash was a good 15 minutes ahead of me as I reached the top, called the Dragon's Tooth. At that point, there was a very steep descent. On my way down, I apparently missed a sharp left turn. My momentum took me sliding on my butt, down this shoot for about 100 yards. I kept on hiking down the path, thinking I was still on the AT. As the path fizzled out, I realized this was not the AT. I was lost, not knowing whether the trail I missed had gone east or west.

This path I had followed had been made by many other hikers who had missed the turnoff as I had done. I had no intention of traveling back up that insane chute. I pulled out my AT guidebook and saw that I was only about a mile from the Four Pines Hostel. My sense of direction told me to continue downhill. I was elated when I eventually saw a country road about 400 yards ahead.

When I finally reached the road, I was relieved to find a lady driving into her driveway. I asked her which direction was the Four Pines Hostel. After she pointed west, I hiked down the road about a mile and arrived just as Crash was arriving from the opposite direction. He laughed, realizing where I had probably missed the trail and reminded me that I was supposed to be following the white blazes.

Joe and Donna Mitchell are owners of the Four Pines Hostel and are wonderful hosts. The hostel was a huge heated garage supplied with many beds and couches, a restroom with showers, a refrigerator with pop and all for a donation at the hiker's discretion. Joe made me feel a little better by informing me that many hikers miss the sharp turnoff coming down that chute, including three hikers earlier that day.

After showers, Eddie, who works at the hostel, shuttled Mountain Man, Animal, Tenderfoot, Crash, and me to an incredible all-you-can-eat meal at the Homeplace Restaurant. It was located in the countryside a couple of miles down the road and originally was a farmhouse. The meal was served family style, and our waitress just kept the food coming. Dessert was an all-you-can-eat peach cobbler. Our hiker appetites were abundantly satisfied. If you like eating, one of the great enjoyments of long-distance hiking is that you can eat as much as you like and never gain any weight. It's a big adjustment and very tough to curb this appetite when a hiker returns home.

The next morning, Four Pines Hostel shuttled most of our gear to our next destination at the Howard Johnson Hotel in Daleville. That meant our packs were only about 5 pounds for our planned 20-mile hike. We were excited as we steadily made progress climbing up to McAfee Knob, the most photographic site on the Appalachian Trail. We were not disappointed. It was a beautiful day with spectacular views. We took an extended snack break at this special spot.

Crash moved ahead of me by a mile when I had to stop for a break. Hiking up to Tinker Cliffs, I missed a sharp turn for the second day in a row. The temperature was in the 70s, and I had run out of water. Luckily, after 30 minutes of bushwhacking through thick brush, I saw a trail far below. I headed down the steep hill and was overjoyed to find those white blazes. A couple of miles further down the trail, I finally arrived at Lamberts Meadow Shelter, dehydrated and exhausted.

Animal was at the shelter, and I asked him how long ago Crash had hiked through. He informed me that he had not arrived as yet. Ten minutes later, here came Crash. He was quite surprised to see me there. He had been waiting for me on top of Tinker Cliffs and eventually gave up on me catching him.

When I got lost, I had somehow passed him without our knowledge. For the second day in a row, he reminded me that I was supposed to be following the white blazes. We laughed, rested, snacked, and drank more than a liter of water at the cold mountain stream in front of the shelter. Eventually we filled our water bottles, and to make sure I was following the white blazes, Crash decided to hike about 50 feet behind me.

The temperature rose to 75 degrees, and we again ran out of water with four miles to go. When we stumbled out of the woods, there was a gas station 100 feet to our right. We made an immediate beeline to the pop machine. Next to the machine was a rack holding coupon books. We found a $39 coupon for the Howard Johnson Hotel, which was next door. The price included an excellent continental breakfast. The hotel was clean and a quiet place to stay. After 12 days of hiking, we registered for two nights.

Usually after about ten days of hiking, we would take a zero day. Our bodies needed the extra day of rest and the extra meals. The problem I had with a day with no hiking was homesickness. My body definitely needed the extra rest, but the extra downtime made me especially miss my wife and the comforts of my life back home.

Arriving in Daleville marked being away from home for a month. Once I started hiking again, most of the homesickness would not surface as much because my mind would become occupied by calculating distances, concentrating on foot placement, planning journal entries, and constantly looking for that next white blaze.

When camping for the night, my mind was busy writing in my journal, checking the next day's terrain, the distances between water sources, possible rest or lunch stops, and our day's destination. All this was accomplished through the help of Appalachian Guidebook, the National Geographic Map books and the Guthook Appalachian Trail GPS App on my iPhone. All three references were always with me.

Down the street about a half mile from our hotel was a strip mall with a nice coffee shop, a well-equipped hiking outfitter store, a restaurant and a barber shop. I spent a lot of time at the coffee shop the next day catching up on my journal. About one out of every ten thru-hikers will journal on www.trailjournals. com. This allows family, friends, and fans to follow along and somewhat take the journey themselves from their homes.

After an extra day's rest and an oatmeal-and-waffle breakfast at the hotel, we left Daleville on Thursday, April 7. The two miles through the Daleville traffic area was a well-planned trail through the trees. The trail then led us through some green cow pastures. Two bulls on the trail graciously allowed us to pass by.

We stopped at Wilson Creek Shelter for lunch. A thru-hiker named Scorched Heels caught up with us just as we were arriving. We visited with him for about ten minutes and then he continued down the trail ahead of us. Fourteen miles into the hike, we crossed the Blue Ridge Parkway for the first time. The AT crosses the parkway many times as the trail parallels the road for many miles.

Exhausted after another 20-mile hike, Crash called the Peaks of Otter Lodge to come and pick us up. The lodge was located on the Blue Ridge Parkway a couple of miles from the trailhead and owned by the National Park Service. The next morning after breakfast, the hotel manager drove us up the Blue Ridge Parkway, and we slack packed 20 miles back to the lodge. We endured many steep ups and downs, and the weatherman threw everything at us that day but the kitchen sink. There was thick fog and cold winds to start with. Next came the rain. The last few miles was a little frightening, hiking under loud thunder, lightning, and pounding hail. We were chilled to the bone when we busted out of the woods at our destination trailhead.

When we got to our room, we turned the heat up to 80 and took long hot showers. This lodge was very nice, and we enjoyed two great evening meals there. In fact, this was the fifth night in a row that we had taken showers and slept in nice comfortable beds. My wife asked me on the phone that night, "Aren't you guys supposed to be camping out?"

I have been told that the Virginia AT offers easier hikes. So far, I was still finding steep mountains to climb. They didn't go up to 6000 feet, but there were still many steep 2000-foot climbs. I did find climbing these heights a little easier. Maybe this was due to acquiring hiker legs, after hiking hundreds of miles.

The next day at daybreak, the Peaks of Otter Lodge shuttled us back to where they had dropped us off the day before, and we then continued northbound. It was 28 degrees, the ground was frozen, but the sky was blue. We had our jackets and gloves on and our ears covered. To stay warm, our pace was brisk. We eventually hiked over the very wide James River on the longest walking bridge on the AT. It was an old railroad bridge that had been converted and upgraded into a very nice walking bridge.

Coming out of the woods, I was awed crossing over the James River on the longest foot bridge on the Appalachian Trail.

Crash decided to hike another ten miles to Punchbowl Shelter. I made a quick trip into Glasgow to pick up a surprise mail drop from Nancy Jack, my daughter-in-law, who lives in Chicago. There was applesauce, yogurt, dried cherries, crackers, health bars, chocolate, and even wine. I ate a meal of it, packed what I had room for, and took the rest over to a nearby shelter to share with three AT hikers who were spending the night there.

Ken Wallace, my shuttle driver, only charged $10 to take me into Glasgow and return me to the trail two hours later. Glasgow had a great shelter with showers that was near the post office, a pizza place, and a grocery store. After Ken took me back to the trailhead, I hiked two more miles up the trail to spend the night at John Hollow Shelter.

Being the only person there, I went to sleep at 8:00 p.m. with the help of a couple of Tylenol PMs. I woke up at 4:00 a.m. and was concerned about snow and a cold front that was forecast. I packed up and left with my headlamp on at 4:30 a.m., hoping to get over Bluff Mountain before the cold weather hit.

Over Bluff Mountain, I became very nervous about my feet, hiking in freezing temperatures on the frozen trail.

As soon as I reached the top of the first steep 2000-foot climb, it started snowing and blowing. For the next ten miles, my hiking legs found a new gear. At the summit of Bluff Mountain, the cold wind seemed to go right through me. I stopped for a moment to take in the view as I took a few swigs of my now slush Gatorade.

The chill factor had to have been in the single digits. As I hiked down from Bluff Mountain, it gradually warmed. After the 20-mile hike, I reached US 60 at 1:00 p.m. and hitched a nine-mile ride into Buena Vista. Crash had already checked in at the Budget Inn. He had hiked the ten miles from Punchbowl Shelter earlier that morning. We were sharing a room for two nights, waiting out the cold weather, replenishing lost calories, resting our weary bodies, and watching the last two days of the Masters Golf Tournament. Life is sometimes good on the Appalachian Trail.

Spring was beginning to show its colors. Besides being surrounded by more greenery, I started seeing colorful butterflies fluttering around as I hiked down the trail. After hiking 860 miles on the AT, I was feeling much more confident about hiking long distances. This section hike, which started in Hot Springs at mile 275, was the longest I had hiked without an injury.

CHAPTER 7

Northern Virginia–
West Virginia–Maryland

**"Wherever we go in the mountains,
we find more than we seek."
—John Muir**

On Monday, April 11, Crash and I were shuttled nine miles back to the trail by Ken Wallace. Immediately there was a 3000-foot climb to the summit of Bald Knob. We were rewarded with some spectacular 360-degree views on a beautiful day. From the summit, it was a fairly easy trail to the Seeley Woodworth Shelter for the night. We were joined by two young hikers named Cosmo and Atlas.

The next day, Cosmo and Atlas were still asleep when we left at daybreak. It was an easy seven-mile trek along the ridgeline to the summit of Priest Mountain. After lunch on top, we took our time and enjoyed a steep but scenic descent off the Priest. After another climb, our 15-mile hike ended for the night at the Harpers Creek Shelter. Cosmo and Atlas eventually joined us for a second night.

In the morning, we immediately climbed 1800 feet over rocks, boulders, and more rocks to the summit of Three Ridges

Mountain. There was a nice view looking back at the Priest. Six miles into the hike, we stopped at Maupin Field Shelter for lunch. Cosmo and Atlas passed by, and they informed us that they were going to hike 19 more miles into Waynesboro. That meant their hike that day totaled 27 miles. Crash and I found out later that this fast and long hike caused them both a few extra days of rest.

Crash and I continued nine more miles to a campsite near the summit of Humpback Mountain. We sat on ledges overlooking impressive vistas as we ate our dinners of steak jerky, cheese, and a Snickers bar for dessert. Waynesboro was ten miles away.

The next day was a much-needed town day, so we were up early and made good time arriving in Waynesboro at noon. We decided to stay at the Quality Inn, which is near the post office, Kroger Grocery, Ming Gardens, and a laundry facility. It was the largest town we have been in, with an estimated population of 15,000. As soon as we showered, we headed to Ming Garden, a fantastic all-you-can-eat buffet where we spent two hours enjoying an enormous amount of food. We were looking forward to the next day's hike when we would enter the Shenandoah National Park.

Under blue skies, our shuttle driver delivered us back to the trail at 7:30 a.m. It was a beautiful day, but the hike to Blackrock Hut was a constant up-and-down 20-mile challenge. The shelters in the Shenandoah National Park are referred to as huts. Just in front of this hut, there was spring water gushing out of a pipe and immediately disappearing back into the ground. I must compliment the trail designers for wisely routing the AT to pass by so many water sources. It is greatly appreciated, especially on those hot and humid days.

Crash and I left Blackrock Hut at daybreak. The sky was blue, and we were soon rewarded with beautiful views at the summit of Blackrock Mountain. I pictured small rolling hills in the Shenandoah Park. They were not small rolling hills. They are still mountains. We climbed and descended these mountains on the

AT all day long. Eight miles into the hike, I stopped at the Loft Mountain Wayside for a hamburger and two thirst-quenching milkshakes. Crash skipped it and continued hiking.

Waysides are convenience stores in the park that are strategically located about 20 miles apart along Skyline Drive. The AT always seemed to be routed near each wayside. The waysides were stocked with gifts, camping supplies, snacks and contained a restaurant that served breakfast, lunch, and dinner. The cheeseburgers and milkshakes were so good, especially to hungry and thirsty hikers.

I eventually finished the 21-mile hike, reaching Hightop Hut at 6:00 p.m. Crash had arrived about an hour earlier, and we enjoyed the company of a fun group of five hikers from Maryland, all tenting nearby the shelter. They had been friends for years and enjoyed hiking together on weekends.

This past week, each day and night has increased in temperature. This gave us more reason to leave camp at daybreak when the temperature was cooler. The trail the next day took us by the Lewis Mountain Campground. There was a camp store there that had Gatorade and snacks, so we stopped for lunch. From there, we were able to make great time and arrived at the Big Meadows Wayside at 4:00 p.m.

We relaxed outside on the lawn eating our hamburgers and milkshakes in the 70-degree sunshine. Big Meadows, the largest wayside in the park, is very popular and a beautiful area. Many people had driven there and were enjoying a Sunday outing around the premises. We eventually hiked down to their very large campsite and self-registered. After setting up our tents, we took showers at the restroom facilities.

The showers were coin operated. After depositing three dollars' worth of quarters, I spent a lot of time soaping down. To my surprise, the showers turned off before I was able to completely rinse off. I told myself to be a little quicker the next time I take a coin-operated shower. The campsite area had many travel trailer campers who were occupying many of the hundreds of campsites for the night. Surprisingly for as many people who were there, it was a quiet night.

Crash and I packed up our gear and left Big Meadows by 6:00 a.m. We were in a hurry to hike eight miles to Skyland Resort before their breakfast closed at 10:30 a.m. We arrived at 10:00 a.m. and enjoyed a vegetable-loaded three egg omelet, which came with toast and some nicely grilled and seasoned potatoes. The server kept our 16-ounce cups filled with quality coffee. It was heaven. After breakfast, we lounged out in the courtyard in the warm sun for the next three hours. At 2:00 p.m., it was time to go back in the restaurant for lunch.

Well rested and well fed after two meals, we hiked 11 more miles, arriving at Pass Mountain Hut at 6:00 p.m. We slept well after a very long day.

The next morning, Crash and I were anxious to hit another Shenandoah Wayside for breakfast. After seven miles, we arrived at the Elkwallow Wayside at 9:30 a.m. and enjoyed egg sandwiches and Gatorades at a picnic table outside. Since the AT trail goes higher in many places than the road, a hiker can many times look down at the very curvy Skyline Drive from far above.

The drive offers many pull-offs for spectacular views. It is

Reaching another mountaintop, I looked down onto the Blueridge Parkway and sort of felt like I reigned over it.

very popular with serious speed bicycles, motorbikes, tour buses, and many people driving their cars along the unique road. Skyline Drive connects to the Blue Ridge Parkway for over 400 miles with no red lights for the entire distance through the Appalachian Mountains. Instead of hiking, the drive is an enjoyable way of seeing the southern Appalachian Mountains. After a great one-hour rest stop, Crash and I left Elkwallow Wayside and hiked nine more miles to Hogwallow Flat and found a marginal spot in the woods to set up our tents. There are plenty of owls in the Appalachian Mountains, and they can make some very loud noises all night long. After slipping into our tents, there were two of them far apart, trying to out hoot the other. The sounds were eerie and loudly echoing through the woods. Eventually, they quieted down, or I possibly just fell asleep.

Did the trail really go up this particular mountain just to go around another boulder?

If there is a boulder the size of a minivan or a bus, the trail designers seem to always take you to these monsters. There have been hundreds of these detours, and I am told there are hundreds more ahead. The higher up the mountains, the more rocks and boulders a hiker finds.

Crash and I packed up our gear and were anxious to hike the ten miles into Front Royal, Virginia. As we reached U.S. Route 522, we left the Shenandoah National Park. The past ten days, we had hiked 163 miles. It was time for another zero day to rest our weary bodies. We decided to stay at the Super 8 Motel. Across the street was Spelunkers. This place had fantastic hamburgers and milkshakes. Crash and I were in hog heaven. Also close by was a large grocery store to resupply.

The weather was warm, and the climate had been very dry. There was a very big fire behind us in the Shenandoah Park that was starting to delay hikers. Crash and I had seen the smoke when we were hiking through the early parts of the National Park, but it had now spread to a much larger area. We were lucky to have passed the area before it started causing detours for hikers.

After an extra day of rest, Crash and I hitched a four-mile ride back to the trail at 7:00 a.m. on Friday, April 22. Our first rest stop was five miles up the trail at the Jim and Molly Shelter. The shelter was large and had a covered porch with a couple of very nice handmade wooden chairs to relax in. We ate a couple of bars and visited with four hikers who were breaking camp. Later that day, I observed thousands of white trillium flowers during about a mile stretch of trail. It was quite spectacular. I did not take any pictures because it was lightly raining. I figured there would be many more up the trail. Unfortunately, this was the only place where I found them.

We stopped at the Dicks Dome Shelter 15 miles into our hike to get out of the rain. The shelter was off the trail and down a ravine about 100 yards. Crash and I spent an hour drying out and waiting for the rain to stop. Finally the sun started to show. We checked the weather forecast on our phones. Heavy rain and a large weather system was forecast to move through our area for the entire night. We were also concerned about more hikers who were coming to this tiny shelter for the night. We decided to hike five more miles to a very busy Route 50 at Ashby Gap and hitch a ride to Winchester, Virginia, get a hotel room, and wait out the storm.

Reaching Route 50, we were picked up by a retired gentleman who had been on a day hike on the AT from the north. He drove us around some back roads showing us the beautiful Virginia farmland and countryside. He seemed to enjoy our company and insisted on stopping at his VFW to buy Crash and me a thirst-quenching beverage. He wanted to know all about our adventures, so we obliged him with not too many exaggerations. He eventually took us to a hotel in Winchester.

After registering and taking a shower, we went across the street and ate a hearty meal at a Mexican restaurant. It poured all night and did not stop until 10:00 a.m., just at checkout time. We hired a shuttle driver to take us back to the trail. Our immediate challenge was the dreaded Roller Coaster, a 14-mile section of constant ascents and descents. We found the hike to be viewless and a very exhausting section, but the reward was arriving at the Bears Den hostel at mile 1003. This very unique AT hostel was owned by the AT and efficiently run by volunteers.

What a beautiful place at the top of a mountain. For $30, we received a bunk with sheets, a large towel for showering, soap to do laundry, a medium-size pizza, and a pint of ice cream. There was a very large lounge, dining, and kitchen area for hikers. Another splendid oasis in the woods, perfectly placed after enduring miles of the Roller Coaster.

A soon-to-be grandma named Arachne was there. Crash and I had camped with her five nights earlier at Pass Mountain Hut. She had started her AT hike in Waynesboro and planned on reaching Katahdin in August. Next year she was planning a flip-flop to Georgia and hike north to Waynesboro to complete her 2180 mile hike of the AT. After completing an approximate 700-mile canoe trip from Northern New York to Maine, she wrote a guide for others to follow. Another interesting hiker on the AT.

Crash and I left Bears Den hostel at daybreak on April 24 and hiked 20 miles to Harpers Ferry. It was a beautiful day, and during the hike, we ran into about 100 Sunday day hikers out enjoying the day. Near the end of our hike, we crossed the Shenandoah River Bridge and left behind 550 miles of Virginia. Entering Harpers Ferry, West Virginia at mile 1023, we reached another significant milestone on this journey.

We stopped at the Appalachian Trail Conservatory Headquarters, to visit with the staff and enjoyed a free soda pop. We then hiked downtown and decided to stay at The Town's Inn mountain hostel on Main Street. What a quaint little town, surrounded by some very beautiful countryside. There was a large crowd of people visiting the town on a Sunday afternoon. It was a very unique historic place to visit. We found a place that served great hamburgers and enjoyed visiting with Biscuit and Scrappy, fast hikers whom we had met back at Bears Den hostel the night before.

At the end of this 20 mile hike, it was an enjoyable stroll through Harpers Ferry.

I could see why some thru-hikers call it quits at Harpers Ferry. The train station is right next to downtown. One of the many trains that passes through every day is a passenger train that goes from Washington, D.C., to Chicago and vice versa. It makes it very convenient and tempting for tired and weary hikers to cross the street to the train station and say good-bye to the Appalachian Trail.

After a healthy breakfast of eggs, bacon, toast, and coffee at the hostel, Crash and I left Harpers Ferry at 7:00 a.m. on April 25. We immediately crossed the Potomac River Bridge, left our very short visit to West Virginia, and entered the state of Maryland. We first followed a beautiful trail for about three miles along the river. Next was a 1000-foot climb and, at the top, found the trail to be a little easier than most.

After 18 miles, we came to the Dahlgren Back Pack Campground. This was a nice tenting area that exists right next to the trail that has restrooms, which also included indoor shower facilities. Another mile up the trail was the old Washington Monument Park. A friend of Crash picked us up there, and since we were staying at his house, he fed us and shuttled us back to the trail after a good sleep.

The next day, we hiked 20 miles from the old Washington Monument Park to Pen Mar Park, and, just like that, we were through the 40 miles of Maryland.

CHAPTER 8

Pennsylvania

"Look deep into nature, and then
you will understand everything better."
—Albert Einstein

On April 27, at 7:00 a.m., Crash and I left the Pen Mar Park at mile 1060. The first 18 miles of Pennsylvania had some rock-and-boulder mazes, but mostly an easier trail than most. The hike ended at Caledonia State Park. This large park had numerous pavilions with picnic tables and grills spread out over acres of beautiful pine trees.

The next day, Crash and I departed Caledonia State Park at 8:00 a.m. We soon came to this really nice double shelter and campsite. I was told that some hiking clubs in the area were competing as to which club could erect the more impressive camping area.

As we continued hiking, the trail took us through this long rhododendron tunnel. I saw hundreds of these after leaving Springer Mountain in Georgia, but it had been a couple of hundred miles since I had seen one. Hikers during the hot summer months would be awed when the rhododendrons start blooming.

It was always kind of fun, moving through rhododendron tunnels.

Soon after, it suddenly started pouring. Crash and I immediately stopped, put on our raincoats, and covered our backpacks with rain covers. Along with the rain, the temperature had dropped significantly. Ten miles down the trail, we stopped at Birch Run Shelter to have a snack and try to warm up. Our fingers were so cold, it became difficult to even open the wrapping on a candy bar. We soon decided to hike five more miles to Toms Run Shelter. These conditions were hypothermic, so our pace increased.

We arrived at Toms Run Shelter at 2:00 p.m., soaking wet and chilled to the bone. We did not waste any time jumping up into the three-sided shelter out of the rain. We quickly pulled our dry clothes and sleeping bag out of our backpacks. After stripping out of our wet clothes, we quickly put on the dry clothes. We spread out our sleeping mats and sleeping bags onto the floor. I quickly put on my down socks and hooded Nano Puff® and slipped into my sleeping bag. After about an hour, we were able to get feeling back into our extremities. Two more hikers, Bananas and Bookworm, arrived about 5:00 p.m. in the same frozen state. We were all finally warm and sleeping by 8:00 p.m.

The next morning after taking off all our nice warm dry clothes, we reluctantly slipped on our still wet hiking shorts and shirts. I decided to leave my dry socks on. It was a chilly 40 degrees, so I put my raincoat on and was off. Crash had left ten minutes before me. After about ten steps away from the shelter, it started pouring again. My dry socks were instantly soaked. One mile down the trail, I stopped at the AT halfway sign to take a picture. It was too cold and rainy to dwell on the significance of the distance.

It again became difficult keeping my fingers and hands warm. I decided not to use my hiking poles, so I tucked them underneath my armpits. I then pulled the sleeves of my raincoat down over my fists. This allowed me to wiggle my fingers to encourage circulation. After about an hour, I found myself passing by the Ironmasters Mansion Hostel. We had called the night before, but it was already booked. The hostel was a large brick building built in 1829 as a residence and remodeled in 2010. The Pine Grove General Store was there and offered hikers a chance to consume a half gallon of ice cream in one sitting. The store was not open this early in the morning, so we missed the opportunity to attempt the challenge. We were also too early to visit the Appalachian Museum that we walked by.

As I walked by the hostel, Crash surprised me as he popped out of a public restroom onto the porch with a big smile on his face. There was an indoor heated bathroom with electric hand dryers. We spent the next 15 minutes thawing out our fingers and hands. To add to the delight, there stood a soda machine on the covered porch. Luckily, we had some dollar bills, and both of us were like two kids in a candy store.

After another thirst-quenching break, we endured eight more miles of frigid hiking. Reaching Route 34, we took a 200-yard detour up the road to the Green Mountain Store. The store/deli was a warm welcome oasis. We drank hot coffee while the deli sandwich maker made us subs loaded with meat and veggies.

We eventually called for a shuttle driver who was located in Boiling Springs. He suggested we hike two miles up the trail and he could meet us at Route 94 in an hour. Once there, the shuttle driver drove us five miles down the road to the Allenberry Resort in Boiling Springs, Pennsylvania. They had a hiker special that included a nice warm room with two queen-size beds for $40. After the severe conditions we had hiked through the past two days, the resort conditions were quite a contrast.

That night at dinner at the resort, we ran into Scorched Heels, whom we had not seen for the last 200 miles. He had been there for four days with the stomach flu. He did not look well and told us if he did not feel better the next day, he would be going home. Bananas and Bookworm hiked in later that evening.

In Pennsylvania, crossing 14 miles of farmland, was a pleasant change from the constant hiking in the woods.

On Saturday, April 30, our shuttle delivered Crash and me back to where he had picked us up the day before. The wet cold weather had passed, and we were welcomed back to the trail under a blue sky. Soon we had climbed to another boulder maze at the top of a ridgeline. For several hundred yards, we climbed over and around boulders the size of cars and buses. After about two miles of ups and downs, we descended to flat farmland. The trail then took us through three miles of cornfields. Arriving at Boiling Springs, there were fishermen everywhere located around a large lake as we hiked into town. We stopped for a breakfast of scrambled eggs, ham, toast, and coffee at a restaurant a block from the trail.

After an hour's rest, we continued eight more miles down the AT, over more flat farmland to Carlisle,

Pennsylvania. We checked in at the Days Inn, just a couple of hundred yards down Route 11 from the trail. The Middlesex Diner was right next to the hotel. This restaurant had a large selection of food, served large portions, and had excellent service. After nine straight days of hiking, we decided to take a zero the next day, which meant we were looking forward to a few more meals at the diner.

We were crossing a 14-mile valley to get back to more mountains. We had four more miles of the flat farmland to go. Crash and I left the Day's Inn at 7:00 a.m. on May 2. The 17-mile hike to Duncannon was in thick fog. We were introduced to some of the zillions of rocks found on the trail in Pennsylvania. Crash insisted that I experience staying a night at the Doyle Hotel. It was one of the original Anheuser-Busch hotels, more than 100 years old. I don't think it had ever been remodeled. After registering, we climbed three flights of stairs to our room. The owners loved visiting and serving hikers at their bar and restaurant. We also received a free shuttle to a grocery store to resupply for our next four-day hike. We ate dinner that night at the Doyle. It rained all night, so we were happy to be warm and dry. Staying at the Doyle, Crash believed I had been officially initiated as a hiker on the Appalachian Trail.

Leaving Duncannon, the trail took us across a long bridge over the Susquehanna River. Crossing over the very wide river made me think back to my great-great-grandparents, William and Hannah Jack. For three months around 1820, with the help of two oxen and an Indian guide, they followed the trails alongside the Susquehanna River from Cecil County, Maryland, to Steuben County, New York. They settled near Cameron, New York, where they built a home, farmed, and raised ten children.

Steuben County is where my mom and dad, grandpa and grandma, and great-grandpa and great-grandma, all raised their families as well. As tough as it is hiking this trail, it is nothing compared to hardships they had to endure back then. Thinking about those long ago days made me realize how spoiled I am in this modern-day life. I think if hiking this trail does nothing else, it had better make me better appreciate all the comforts I take for granted.

After crossing the bridge, the trail immediately took us into the woods and up a steep long climb. Once on top of the ridgeline, I was not surprised to find another mile-long boulder maze to maneuver over and around. An 11-mile hike put us at the well-kept Peter's Mountain Shelter, built in 2008. The next shelter was 18 miles away and too far to go any farther. Rain was again forecast for that night, so we decided to deal with it in the morning.

Pennsylvania's AT not only had a lot of rocks but also had a lot of poison ivy along both sides of the trail. Sometimes it grows right on the trail, and other times it reaches out over the trail. We constantly have to watch out for it. Crash and I both wore hiking shorts so we had to be careful. I can see why some hikers wear long pants.

Crash enjoying a rest stop. Every 4 or 5 miles, we would take our packs off, snack and rest our weary bodies. After a 15 minute break, we frequently felt rejuvenated.

Crash and I had been hiking in thick fog for three days. Many times during the day, we heard trains blowing their whistles as they travelled along rivers and valleys far below. It's a pleasant sound as we hike through the quiet of the woods. This has gone on for the past 1200 miles. Train travel is still alive and well in some areas.

I left Peter's Mountain Shelter before Crash and arrived 18 miles later at Rausch Gap Shelter. The day was cloudy, but it was an easier hike, and Crash arrived 20 minutes later. The next day, Crash and I hiked 18 more miles, which had many more ups and downs. We arrived at the 501 Shelter, on Route 501, to find this shelter fully enclosed with 12 bunks. It was owned by the Appalachian Trail and maintained by a caretaker who lived next door. Hikers can order food from a restaurant two miles away that delivers to the shelter. Crash and I each ordered a large pizza for dinner and a sub sandwich for the next day's hike.

For four days, Crash and I had been hiking northbound and had met Captain Kirk and Swamp Angel going southbound. The second day I saw them, I said, "Didn't we pass each other yesterday going in opposite directions?" Then they explained what they were doing. They had two cars, one parked where they started southbound and the other parked where they finished the day's hike. After a night at a motel, they then drove their car much farther north and hiked southbound again to the car they had left the day before. They were moving northbound, but hiking each day southbound. They started this section hike in Duncannon and were planning to continue this section hike routine all the way to Connecticut. This is another unique method of hiking the AT.

Crash and I left the 501 Shelter at daybreak. Shortly after, it started raining hard. We became drenched and chilled to the bone again. To stop meant to become hypothermic. The 24-mile hike was wet, cold, and seemed like it would never end. It was simply a very challenging day to endure. We were extremely tired and relieved when we busted out of the woods into Port Clinton.

We registered at the Port Clinton Hotel that was a block down from the trail. We were surprised to find Scorched Heels there. He had recovered from the stomach flu and had been a half day ahead of us since leaving Boiling Springs, 100 miles back.

After showers, we enjoyed an incredible prime rib dinner at the hotel. After dinner, I did laundry in the basement of the hotel. Later at the bar, we were visiting with a very nice couple who graciously offered to give us a two-mile ride to Walmart to resupply. They also waited for us and drove us back to the hotel.

After a good night's sleep, we hiked up a pretty steep hill

There was plenty of this terrain to endure in Pennsylvania, better known on the trail as Rocksylvania.

out of Port Clinton to start our planned 15-mile hike for the day. One of the day's highlights was hiking up and over boulders to Pulpit Rock. There was a very nice view of the valley below and a great spot for a snack break. The next eight miles was a nice smooth trail to the Eckville Shelter at mile 1228. Crash was about a mile in front of me. Not realizing it, I missed the turnoff and hiked another mile up the trail. I know what you are thinking: *Not again.*

I knew I should have reached the shelter, so I finally stopped, pulled out my AT guidebook, and saw that I had passed the turnoff. I was in a swampy area, and the next shelter was too far away, so I backtracked the mile and saw where I had missed the turnoff. Usually there is a very visible sign posted pointing in the direction of a shelter, but the sign was almost impossible to see. Another two more miles of extra credit.

Crash and I left Eckville Shelter at 7:00 a.m. on May 8. Two miles of climbing and we reached the top of a ridgeline where we encountered a very challenging trail of jagged rocks for a five-mile stretch. It was a treacherous area for a potential ankle injury. It was slow hiking and a tiring section to endure. Seven miles into the hike, we were exhausted and took a 30-minute snack break at the Allentown Shelter.

We found the next four miles to be much smoother. About 2:00 p.m., at mile 1240, we came to Route 309, and 200 yards down the road, the restaurant at the Blue Mountain B&B was open. You know what that meant? *Food.* It was Mother's Day, and the restaurant was crowded. It would be a long wait, but we didn't mind as long as they continued filling our glasses with soda pop.

Inside we met a group of five hikers having a very good time: Mountain Man; his wife Karma, from Switzerland; Smudgy Cheeks; his sister, Bubbles; and her husband, Sprout. They had all started their thru-hike 220 miles back in Harpers Ferry. They planned on completing the north section of the AT and then bus back to Harpers Ferry. They then planned to head southbound to Georgia. Many hikers are following this flip-flop pattern. The AT organization promotes this to help spread out the hikers along the trail. We all enjoyed filling up on hamburgers and fries.

After a great lunch break, hiking the next six miles to Bake Oven Knob Shelter was very challenging. There was a two-mile ridgeline of boulder mazes that required careful maneuvering over and around. Two of the areas were called Knife Edge and Bear Rocks. We managed to arrive at the shelter without any injuries.

The five hikers we had met at the restaurant all eventually wandered in one at a time. They all set up tents while Crash and

I rested on our sleeping bags in the shelter. After getting settled, the five came over, cooked their meals, and ate dinner at the picnic table right in front of the shelter. They were having fun and really enjoying each other's company. Mountain Man showed us a picture of a copperhead snake that his wife, Karma, had almost stepped on about eight miles back. I also heard Karma proudly and casually mentioning to her group that she had not cried that day. It was a most entertaining evening listening to them reminiscing about their day's hike.

A fun group from left to right, Mountain Man, Smudgy Cheeks, Sprout, Bubbles and Karma.

The next two days we experienced easier 15-mile hikes each day to Wind Gap, Pennsylvania. One of those days as I hiked through the stillness of the woods, I was frightened by a loud rustling explosion nearby, that caused my heart to skip a couple of beats. I slammed on my brakes, turned, and lifted my poles, pointing them at the charging bear to defend myself. To my great relief, I witnessed this very large wild turkey taking flight.

I slept reasonably well at night. The only significant thing that happened in my dreams was a nightmare that occasionally occurred. I would wake up finding myself thrashing about, fighting some Appalachian creature that was attacking me. Crash had mentioned the commotion I sometimes made in the middle of the night.

In Wind Gap, mile 1275, Crash and I shared a room at the Travel Inn. It was a little rundown, but it was next to restaurants, a coin laundry, and a great ice-cream stand. We ate well and were looking forward to a 17-mile hike into Delaware Water Gap for the next day. The soles of my shoes were smooth as glass, so I was also looking forward to a new pair of Altra Olympus hiking shoes hopefully waiting for me at the post office there.

Crash and I hired a cab to take us three miles back to the trail at 6:30 a.m. the next day. It was a rocky trail for most of the hike. Around noon, we came out of the woods at a power line crossing and decided that this was the perfect place to take our lunch break. There was a nice view of the farmland far below. We took our packs off, sat down on the soft grass, and enjoyed our subway sandwiches that we had bought the night before.

Eventually we came out of the woods at Delaware Water Gap, mile 1290, the last town in Pennsylvania. The Deer Head Inn was the first building we came to and decided immediately to stay there. The beautifully remodeled three-story inn was built in 1867. It had been ten days of hiking, so we registered for two nights.

Our first evening in Delaware Water Gap, Crash and I enjoyed a very nice dinner at the Sycamore Grille. We also visited with Rocketman and Princess—thru-hikers whom we had run into for the past three days. They carried a light daypack and hiked in a very unique manner. Captain Kirk and Swamp Angel used two vehicles, but Rocketman and Princess used only one.

Princess would drop her husband, Rocketman, at one end of the day's hike and then she would drive to a road crossing at the opposite end of their day's hike. Thus, they would hike in opposite directions. When Rocketman would get to their car, he would drive to where he started and pick up Princess. They would then find a hotel and eventually find a nice place to chow down. This is hiking the Appalachian Trail in style.

Our second day in Delaware Water Gap marked 69 days that I had been away from home. I took a two-hour hike around the small downtown area to try and ease my homesickness. I eventually called Penny and told her I really wanted to come home. She informed me to hike a couple of more days to think about it. She did not want me coming home and regretting my decision to leave the Trail.

CHAPTER 9

New Jersey and New York

"Nature is saturated with deity."
—Ralph Waldo Emerson

I left Delaware Water Gap, wearing my new Altra Olympus shoes just before daybreak on May 13. I immediately crossed the lighted I-80 bridge over the Delaware River. Thank goodness there was a railing separating hikers from the busy traffic zooming by at 80 mph. I was glad to leave over 220 miles of Pennsylvania's rocks and boulders. As I crossed the very long bridge, I counted over 30 hawks soaring all over the sky. It was a fascinating site as they welcomed me to New Jersey.

After crossing the bridge, the trail went back into the woods. The white blazes led me up 1200 feet to the large Sunfish Pond. Around the pond, the trail was filled with huge rocks and lots of bushes. Maneuvering around the shoreline was a chore. This little section made me nervous because this area was known for rattlesnakes. I did not see any as I slowly circled the pond, but probably stepped over a few dens of them. Ten miles into the hike, Crash caught up to me as I came to a road crossing that led to the Mohican Outdoor Shelter. We took our first rest stop at the road and enjoyed some snacks. It started raining, so we put on our rain gear and continued hiking.

We continued keeping our eyes glued to the trail passing Rattlesnake Spring and Rattlesnake Mountain. I did see a black snake on the trail and played with it awhile with my hiking pole. Crash and I hiked in thick fog and hard rain the last 15 miles. Arriving at Brink Shelter, I was soaking wet and very tired from the long 25-mile hike. I decided to spend the night there.

Three other hikers were already at the small shelter, so Crash decided to hike three more miles to U.S. Route 206 and get a motel. We decided to meet at that road crossing the next morning at 7:00 a.m. I stripped down, put on some dry clothes, and found a spot for my pad and sleeping bag. I visited with Snipe, Marshall Reed, and Wazo, all of whom had started their thru-hike in Harpers Ferry and had hiked 15 miles earlier that day from the Mohican Outdoor Shelter. We were all in our bags and sleeping soon after.

I left the Brink Shelter at 6:00 a.m. while the others were still in their sleeping bags. The three-mile hike to Culvers Gap was brisk. Crash was waiting when I arrived. I hiked 200 yards down the road to a tackle shop to buy a couple of sports drinks. We hiked 20 miles that day to County Road 519. We found the phone number for the High Point Country Inn from our guidebook. Crash called the manager, and he soon picked us up and took us two miles down the road to his very clean motel. After showers, we ordered pizza and soda pop that was delivered to our room.

The highlight of the hike today was stopping at High Point Park Headquarters where we were fortunate to have some trail magic from Plank and his wife. Plank had hiked the AT the previous year. They live in Connecticut and were driving south for a couple of hundred miles, stopping at different trailheads to generously offer their snacks and drinks to hikers along the AT.

The next morning, we hiked six miles and then took Lott Road a short distance into the small village of Unionville. As we walked down Main Street, the Sunday church bells were ringing as people were entering the church. Down the street, we stopped at the Horler's General Store for breakfast. Crash and I sat on their porch enjoying an egg-and-sausage sandwich and some coffee. Three miles up the road, we saw a pair of swans as we hiked around a large bird refuge. Entering the woods again, there was a short climb up Pochuck Mountain and a couple of miles later a descent to County Road 517.

As we came out of the woods at this road, there were cars and people everywhere. The Sunday day hikers were walking both directions on this well-built popular boardwalk. This unique boardwalk twisted and turned for over a mile above this marsh area. We reached Route 94 and headed 100 yards down the road to the Heaven Hill Farm and Garden Center. Crash and I enjoyed some ice cream on their porch. We eventually called the Appalachian Motel, which was located a couple of miles down the road.

The next day we were going to be entering New York and were planning a four-day hike. The manager was kind enough to drive us a few miles into Vernon, New Jersey, to resupply. We also bought sub sandwiches for tonight's dinner and a sub for the next day's hike. In the morning, our hike started by a steep climb up Wawayanda Mountain. At the top, Crash and I hiked nine miles of rolling wooded hills. We stopped and took pictures of the state line that was painted on a large boulder, indicating we were leaving New Jersey and entering New York. The past three days, Crash and I covered 70 New Jersey miles. I thought after leaving Pennsylvania, we would see less rocks. It was not the case.

Shortly after passing the state line, we stopped at Prospect Rock where we had a view of the New York City skyline. We decided to sit on the boulders, relax, and enjoy our sub sandwich lunch. Prospect Rock happened to be the highest point on the

AT in New York. Soon after, Crash and I reached Route 17A. We picked our pace up as we hiked 200 yards up the road to the popular Bellvale Farms Creamery. It has been owned by a farming family for the last few generations. We both ordered large hot fudge sundaes and loaded up on orange soda pop. It was another welcome oasis from the woods.

After a very enjoyable break, we hiked up the trail two more miles, arriving at Wildcat Shelter at 4:00 p.m. Bananas was there resting in her hammock. We had not seen her since Boiling Springs, 250 miles back. We enjoyed our time talking to her about where we had seen hikers that we were both familiar with. Several more section hikers arrived before dark. After eating some cheese, a bag of steak jerky, and some trail mix for dessert, I slipped into my sleeping bag and passed out about 7:00 p.m.

It looked like a sunny day, as Crash and I left Wildcat Shelter at daybreak. We were expecting a challenging day of steep climbs up and over rocks and boulders. It was more dangerous and exhausting than the day before. I asked Crash, "Are these states in competition to see which one can create the most

During the first 35 miles of New York, it became monotonous, struggling up countless of these rock and boulder climbs.

difficult trail?" He responded by saying, "There may be something to that."

After 16 miles, Crash and I arrived at Fingerboard Shelter. We set up our tents in a grassy area nearby. Bananas arrived about an hour later, and she decided to stay in the shelter. Several more hikers arrived and set up tents. It was a pleasant night with no wind. Crash enjoyed a cigar, celebrating our completing two-thirds of the AT. We were looking forward to reaching Bear Mountain the next day.

As we left Fingerboard Shelter at daybreak on May 18, the sky was partly cloudy, and the forecast projected a pleasant 70 degrees for the day. After 12 miles, we were rewarded at the top of Bear Mountain with soda and snack vending machines.

Bear Mountain is a very popular to climb for locals. People may also drive to the top on a paved road. There is a stone lookout tower with spectacular views in every direction. We had camped with Bananas and Hap the past two nights. Hap's two-week section hike would end here. The four of us took a needed break. The first 36 miles of New York had been brutal. We relaxed on a bench and enjoyed the nice breeze and the company. It was a special time, since we all felt that we had reached another milestone.

We were all experiencing a great feeling of accomplishment, conquering the first 35 relentless miles of New York and reaching the summit of Bear Mountain.

I felt reaching Bear Mountain was a milestone. I was overwhelmed, looking down on the Hudson River and the Bear Mountain Bridge.

Leaving the top of Bear Mountain, I was very impressed with three-feet-wide stone steps that a company meticulously had positioned all the way down the mountain. Crash informed me that it had taken them three years to complete. At the base of the mountain, people were spread out everywhere enjoying Bear Mountain Park.

We continued to move slowly through this very massive park filled with picnic tables, benches, and large trees. The AT continued through the park and eventually led us through the Bear Mountain Zoo. Compared to climbing up and over rocks, boulders, and mountains the last couple of months, this was the most enjoyable stroll.

Near the end of the park, we were rewarded again to find an ice-cream-vending machine. My favorite ice-cream bar is an ice-cream sandwich. I was overjoyed to see that one of the choices was a jumbo ice-cream sandwich. I could not put my $3 in fast enough. Instead, to my horror, out came a bright-red-and-yellow sponge-bob Popsicle. I shouted, "You've got to be kidding me." Every time Crash and Bananas looked over at me eating this colorful delight, they would burst out laughing.

Feeling rested, we leisurely continued hiking over the Hudson River crossing the Bear Mountain Bridge. Far below we could see and hear trains coming and going on both sides of the river. After crossing, we had to shift gears for another steep climb. On top of the ridge, the trail became kind, and we quickly covered the last six miles to Route 9.

There was a very busy 24-hour gas station and convenience store at the road crossing. Several hikers were there, including Tenderfoot, whom we had not seen for the past 660 miles. We spent 30 festive minutes at the very busy store reminiscing and chowing down. Crash's son showed up, who lives in the area. Crash was going to spend a few days with him. After introductions, it was time for Crash and me to say our good-byes.

After spending 65 days together on the AT, we found ourselves embracing one another. He had been my guide, companion, friend, and mentor through all the challenges of the past 1000 miles. I suddenly found myself a little emotional as I began hiking up the trail alone. A mile later, I came to the Graymoor Monastery camping pavilion. It had been a long 20-mile hike. I laid awake a long time, reminiscing about Crash and our two months of hiking and camping with one another.

I had wanted to leave the trail since Delaware Water Gap, where Crash and I took our last zero. My wife had advised me to take two more days to think about it. Instead, I had taken seven days debating this, and it always ended with *It's time to go home.* I decided that my section hike would end when I reached the train station in Pawling, New York. I would hike two more days to get there.

The weather forecasters were calling for temperatures for the next week to be in the high 80s. I did not do well, hiking in that kind of heat. This was another confirmation for me that I was making the right decision to go home. I missed my wife and my home and felt guilty about her being alone. The summer climate in Anchorage is quite delightful, and I was anxious to experience it again. I had lost 20 pounds, and that was probably another good reason to go home and start eating a lot healthier.

I left the Graymoor pavilion at 6:00 a.m. Crash caught up with me four miles into my hike. I thought we had said our good-byes the night before at the convenience store. I was surprised and glad to see him. For the next several miles, we enjoyed each other's company. We reminisced about the miles we had hiked, camped, laughed, and lived our AT experiences together. I was the benefactor of his companionship. I was blessed to have experienced his enthusiasm for hiking and his wealth of information about the AT.

We also discussed, for the final time, my decision to leave the trail. He finally said to me, "Whatever you decide will be the right decision." He could have made me feel guilty by trying to talk me into staying, but chose to let it be my decision. Crash grew up hiking in the White Mountains in New Hampshire with his brother. Hiking was in his blood. He had legs that could easily power up the steepest mountains. He loved the challenges that the Appalachian Trail provided.

At the RPH Shelter at mile 1425, we embraced again, and he headed back to his son's family home. I rested there for about an hour, dwelling on Crash's exit. I decided to hike nine more miles to the Morgan Stewart Shelter. Just before leaving the RPH shelter, someone coming down the trail yelled, "Holcomb." As I turned, I was surprised to see Boomerang and his girlfriend hiking in. The last time I had seen him, we were hiking out of the Partnership Shelter, 900 miles back. There, he had brought us half a gallon of ice cream and a large bag of homemade oatmeal cookies. I often ran into a familiar hiker whom I hadn't seen for weeks at a time. It happens to all long-distance hikers on the AT.

After a short visit, I departed. Nine miles later, I arrived at Morgan Stewart Shelter. I met another thru-hiker and senior citizen named Turtle. He started a campfire and I enjoyed talking with him. He was solo hiking and seemed relaxed and well grounded. When I mentioned I was ending my hike 12 miles up the trail at Pawling, he tried to talk me into continuing. I still found it tempting. Just as it was getting dark, Boomerang showed up, and we were able to catch up on many of the highlights of our AT adventure.

I left the Morgan Stewart Shelter at 6:00 a.m. on Friday, May 20. I was anxious to go home, so it was a brisk pace hiking the 12 miles to the train in Pawling. I was leaving the trail after completing a total of 1500 miles. I was feeling good about accomplishing 1175 miles on my fourth section hike of the AT. I was lucky to have run into Crash. He definitely helped me through the past 1000 miles. For the first time since starting to hike the AT 15 months ago, I was returning home without an injury.

The train ride was about 90 minutes to Grand Central Station. During the ride, I experienced a very strange feeling, leaving the quiet isolation of the woods and heading back to the hustle and bustle of civilization. Emerging from the train into Grand Central Station, I felt a little like an alien, out of place in a strange new world. It was an incredible contrast from the woods, to a Friday afternoon on 42nd Street in New York City. I eventually found a bus to JFK. I boarded an Alaska Airlines flight to Seattle, then on to Anchorage. I was very anxious to see my wife after being absent for 78 days. When our eyes met, we rushed to one another, and our long bear-hug embrace said it all.

CHAPTER 10

Connecticut and Massachusetts

"Silence is the source of great strength."
—Lao Tzu

After 11 months at home, Spring had arrived, and I was ready to return to Pawling to continue my trek northbound. On Saturday, April 15, 2017, I flew from Anchorage to Newark. After arriving, I took the standing-room-only train from the Newark Airport, which traveled under the Hudson River, to Penn Station in New York City. I then hiked several very crowded blocks to Grand Central Station to find a train to Pawling, New York. The streets were ridiculously packed with people for Easter weekend. Honking cars and buses added to the chaos. I couldn't get out of New York City fast enough. I felt better and much more at ease as the train headed north, away from the bustle and noise of Manhattan.

I love riding on a train, and there were not many passengers this time of night. After two and a half hours, I arrived in Pawling at 10:00 p.m. I fetched my headlamp out of my backpack and hiked a mile to the Pawling Park where I set up my tent and spent the night near a large pavilion. I was so tired from the 15 hours of travel, I slipped into my tent and soon fell asleep.

The next morning I packed up and hiked three miles back to the trail. The temperature was 80 degrees, a little warmer than I had anticipated this time of year. After hiking five miles, I made a half-mile detour down Route 22 to Tony's Deli for lunch. The sandwiches they make there are out of this world. The New York accents of the workers made this break a very special and unique rest stop. I ate a delicious Italian sub with the works. I added a sub and a couple of sport drinks to my supplies to take with me.

Back on the trail, I met many day hikers out enjoying the beautiful day. Coming from 40-degree temperatures in Alaska, my body was having a hard time adjusting to the extreme change in temperature. It was a tiring 14-mile hike for my first day back; however, I felt good as I arrived at the Wiley Shelter at 4:00 p.m. I set up my tent on one of the tent platforms and then quenched my thirst with my last sport drink.

Two local school teachers arrived, who were heading southbound. They informed me that every Spring break they hike a section of the AT with their dogs. About 6:00 p.m., two northbound thru-hikers arrived, having hiked 25 mile that day. Lumberjack and Young Blood had left Springer Mountain in January and February, respectively. At 7:00 p.m., it started raining, and I headed for my tent. The next morning, Lumberjack and Young Blood left camp at 7:00 a.m. Most young hikers are on more of a budget than most retiree hikers. I think that is one of the reasons that younger hikers feel they may have to log more miles per day.

I left Wiley Shelter after the sun and wind had dried out my tent from the night's rain. Shortly into the hike, I left New York and crossed into Connecticut. Nine states down, five more to go. I enjoyed a comfortable pace along a very scenic stretch of trail that paralleled a loud cascading stretch of the Housatonic River.

After a few miles of this, I stopped at the covered Bulls Bridge. I hiked up a hundred yards to the Bulls Bridge Country Store and enjoyed an apple, an ice-cream sandwich, and a Gatorade. I continued hiking about five more miles to Kent along the scenic Housatonic River. I decided to stay at the Fife 'n Drum Inn for the night. The railroad tracks were only ten feet from the building. I didn't notice this until the middle of the night, when a train came blasting through. I suddenly sat up out of a deep sleep, thinking I was experiencing another Alaskan earthquake. The bed literally shook me for ten minutes until the train finally passed. Thank goodness that was the only train that came through that night.

I crawled out of bed around 8:00 a.m. and wandered across the street to the Villager Restaurant and had a hearty breakfast of eggs, potatoes, bacon, and my first coffee in a few days. I went back to my room and rested till checkout at 11:00 a.m. The trail continued to take me along a beautiful trail next to the Housatonic River. The weather provided blue skies and 70-degree temperatures.

At Caesar Brook Campsite, a blue blaze trail led me to this welcoming site in the woods.

I met only two hikers that day. Everyone seems to have a story on the AT. Jordon had been saving up money the past couple of years so he could hike the AT. Three weeks ago he called Steve, who lived several hundred miles away. They had known one another during their college years. He asked Steve over the phone if he had a girlfriend. Steve replied no. Jordon then convinced Steve to join him on his 2180-mile trek. They had just started in Massachusetts and were heading southbound. When they finished in Georgia, they planned to do a flip-flop back to Massachusetts and head north from there. We shared some trail information and soon went in opposite directions.

I ended the very relaxing and peaceful ten-mile hike by huffing and puffing up a very steep half-mile climb to a very unique Silver Hill Campsite. The large campsite had a nice bench swing, picnic tables, and a small pavilion. I set up my tent, boiled water on my one-ounce pop-can stove, and cooked a delicious Mary Jane Farm dehydrated Shepherd's Pie dinner. After hanging my food bag on a high limb away from my tent, I was ready for sleep.

The next day I was welcomed back to the Appalachian Trail. It was a tough 14-mile hike to the Sharon Mountain Campsite. There were many steep ups and downs over rocks and rough terrain. It beat me up. Halfway through the hike, I stopped at a stream to drink and fill my water bottle. Coming down the trail southbound, a gal stopped, and we visited for a while. Her trail name was Charmin. Charmin was slack-packing with only about a four-pound pack. She had completed about 600 miles of the AT over many years. Her hope was to eventually finish the 2180 miles of the AT.

Her husband had dropped her off at an AT trailhead several miles back. His plan was to find a golf course. After his round of golf, he would pick her up at the other end of her hike. They were from Ohio and had just come from Boston where their son had run in the Boston Marathon. She had five miles to go and was looking forward to their wedding-anniversary dinner that evening. She was the only hiker I saw all day.

At 4:00 p.m., it started raining. Luckily, I was passing by the Sharon Mountain Campsite and immediately made a beeline for a tent site that was next to the trail. I set my tent up in record time and somehow managed to keep my sleeping bag and all my gear dry during the process. Shortly after settling into my sleeping bag, I was startled when my phone rang. It was Crash. The reception was unusually clear, and a call from Crash was a huge surprise. He asked me, "Where are you?" I told him Sharon Mountain Campsite, a few miles from Falls Village. We laughed and visited for about 15 minutes. He eventually wished me safe hiking, and all of a sudden, the only noise was the rain hitting my tent. As I comfortably lay there, many memories came back from our 1000-mile hike from the previous year. It made me miss his company.

I was tired and slept well that night. At 6:00 a.m., I woke to find the rain had stopped. I was anxious to have breakfast at the Toymakers Cafe in Falls Village, so I was soon off. It was a short seven-mile hike, and I arrived at 9:30 a.m. Owners Greg and Annie are hiker friendly. They allow hikers to tent on their property near their cafe. After a hearty breakfast, I decided to take half a day off and rest my weary body after the previous day's grueling hike. It allowed me to go to the library and catch up on my journal. The library was a couple of houses down from the cafe.

Falls Village claims to be the smallest town in Connecticut—at least that's what the sign said when I came into town. That night, I had a great fish-and-chip dinner down the street at the Falls Village Inn. After dinner, I walked the short distance back to the Toymakers Cafe and crawled into my tent just as it started raining. I sleep better in my tent than in the shelters, especially with the sound and rhythm of rain hitting the tent.

The next day, the rain stopped about daybreak. I crawled out of my tent and wandered over to the Toymakers Cafe for another great

A hearty breakfast or lunch can be found in Falls Village at the Toymaker's Café.

organic breakfast of veggies and eggs. Greg and Annie have a very unique mom-and-pop place for breakfast and lunch. It is a great eatery near the trail for hikers.

After packing up, I hiked 400 yards back to the trail. Somehow I missed the white blaze where it entered the woods. After backtracking a half mile, I found my mistake. There was an immediate climb up to the very top of Prospect Mountain. I felt stronger that day, and I knew those three meals I had in Falls Village provided me with the fuel and energy that the Appalachian Trail requires. Once on top, I sat down on a large boulder and took in the view.

After a snack and a couple of swigs of ginger ale, I was back hiking. I was in no hurry that day, so my slower pace allowed me to enjoy my surroundings. The trail had some minor ups and downs but was unexpectedly smooth for the AT. I stopped to take a picture of a large unique upright rock called the Giants Thumb. The forest was full of pine trees throughout most of this hike. It was a very peaceful and therapeutic walk and one of the most enjoyable hikes I have had over the 1600 miles on the AT. I decided to spend the night at a hostel in Salisbury, next to restaurants and a grocery store.

The next morning, I felt a little mole on the right side near my waist. It was difficult to turn my head to see it. I looked closer and noticed this little mole had tiny legs. I had a tick embedded in me. The angle made it difficult to get it out. I went downstairs and showed the owner of the hostel. To my surprise, she immediately grabbed the tick and yanked it out. I asked her if she got the head, and she insisted she did. She said it was a dog tick. She had two house dogs, and I assumed that the tick had found me in bed. I figured the tick had only found me several hours ago, so there was no large circles developing. After putting some triple antibiotic cream

Many times there were no views at mountain tops on the AT, but Mount Race was an exception. I consistently felt rewarded, reaching the top of a mountain with a view.

on the wound, I hit the trail. I decided to check on it every day and watch for signs of Lyme disease.

Six miles into the hike, I started climbing up Bear Mountain. It seems like every AT state has a Bear Mountain. It was Sunday, and there were hundreds of day hikers out enjoying the 70-degree temperatures. There was an incredible view at the 2300-foot summit. A mile down the other side, I came to a raging creek in Sages Ravine. The trail followed the scenic ravine for about a mile. After crossing the stream, it was a gradual climb up to the summit of Mount Race. There were a lot of ledges at the top and more spectacular views of the surrounding area.

After a gradual descent, I struggled up a very steep climb to Mount Everett, which offered no views. The Hemlock Shelter was only a mile away, where I had planned to spend the night. The 16-mile hike, with all its spectacular views, helped make this tough hike an enjoyable one.

The next morning, I was up early for a hike into Sheffield, Massachusetts. My retired dentist from Anchorage was due to arrive in Sheffield at 12:30 p.m. on Peter Pan Bus lines from New York City. After crossing into Massachusetts, I arrived there just in time to watch him get off the bus. Doc had called me about a month ago and asked me if he could join me on the AT this year. He had hiked 500 miles on the Camino in Spain the previous year, so I knew he had some long-distance hiking under his belt. I was glad to have some company and someone to share motel expenses with.

We then walked over to Jess Treat B&B, where we had reservations for the night. After settling in, Doc and I walked a couple of blocks to the Marketplace Cafe for lunch. I had an incredible roast-beef sandwich with caramelized onions and peppers, with horseradish spread on multigrain bread. Doc ordered a chicken curry wrap. The sandwiches were so good that we had them make duplicates so we could take them with us for lunch on the AT the next day.

They wrapped them up and put them in cute little brown paper bags. Jess allowed us to put them in her refrigerator to keep them fresh. Later that night for dinner, we went down the street to the Bash Bish restaurant and had some of the best pizza I have ever eaten. We were definitely fueled up for the next day's hike.

Jess made a great breakfast for us. Her son, Kai, does shuttling for hikers, so we hired him to drive us to the trail. After a couple of cups of coffee for breakfast, Doc's adrenaline had spiked, and he was ready to start running up the first mountain. I mentioned that I would be leading up the first climb.

Eventually we reached the very picturesque Tom Leonard Shelter around noon for lunch. We had been salivating all morning, thinking about those sandwiches that the Marketplace Cafe had meticulously made and wrapped for us the day before. We took off our packs, unzipped our lunch compartment, and then realized that we both had left our sandwiches in Jess's refrigerator. Frustrated, we settled for some boring trail snacks, and after about a 20-minute break, we were on our way.

An hour later, we came out of the woods and crossed Route 23. I could not stop thinking about those sandwiches. I finally

Kai serving lunch.

pulled out my cell phone and called Kai. I asked him if he could shuttle our sandwiches to Route 23. He informed me he could have them there in 15 minutes and that the shuttle would cost us $20. I told him we would be waiting. Doc was pleasantly surprised when he heard me talking to Kai. We found a spot for our all-of-a-sudden rest stop. When Kai arrived, he exited his car with a smile as he held up the two brown paper bags. After thanking Kai, Doc and I happily indulged in the most enjoyable and expensive sandwiches we had ever eaten.

We then continued several more miles to the South Wilcox Shelter. Just as we arrived, it started raining. I put on my rain gear and backtracked 200 yards to a mountain stream to fill our water bottles. Doc had brought his efficient one-pound jet boil cooking system. He boiled water, and we had hot chocolate to warm us up. The wind started howling, and the temperature dropped to around 40-degrees as we slipped into our sleeping bags for the night. We were glad to be out of the downpour.

I did not sleep well; however, Doc was snoring as soon as he laid his head down. In the morning, we took our time packing up, hoping the rain would stop. Doc again boiled water, and we enjoyed a cup of hot coffee to warm up. We finally decided to start hiking in the rain. By noon, we were tired of the miserable cold rain. At the next road crossing, we decided to hitch a ride a few miles into Lee, Massachusetts. Once we got a ride, we had the driver drop us off at the Super 8. Lee was a large town with many restaurants. We did our laundry and enjoyed two great meals that day.

The next morning after a hearty breakfast at Rose's Restaurant, Doc and I hired a cab to take us six miles back to the trail. The temperature was 60 degrees, and it had stopped raining. Perfect hiking conditions. The highlight of the hike was going an extra mile to check out the Upper Goose Pond Cabin and take our lunch there. We were glad we did. What a beautiful place.

The large bright-red cabin could house many hikers and had a large covered porch with a picnic table. There were many more picnic tables scattered throughout the many tent sites. There was also a dock area for waterfront activities. The campsite was closed until sometime in May, but we enjoyed some great turkey sandwiches that the 51 Restaurant had made for us the night before.

We eventually headed back to the White-Blazed Trail and soon reached a walking bridge over I-90. There were two huge signs for traffic heading east or west, informing traffic that they were driving under the Appalachian Trail walking bridge. Like young kids, we stood on the bridge over the highway for about five minutes, giving the numerous semitrucks the up-and-down arm motion to honk their blow horns. Most all of them did. Obviously, we had been in the woods too long. After our little fun, we wandered over a few hundred yards to the Berkshire Lakeside Inn. We had reservations and mail drops there and ordered pizza delivery that night.

Doc and I left Berkshire Lodge at 8:00 a.m., with an immediate climb up to the summit of Becket Mountain. Once on the ridgeline, we continued hiking through pine trees for seven miles to the October Mountain Shelter. We arrived to find five middle-aged hikers who were there for the night.

This local group does a weekend hike together every fall and spring. They cut up a lot of firewood from trees that had already fallen and help maintain the area where they decide to camp. They were a fun group that had known each other for years and enjoyed camping and hanging out together. Doc and I set up our tents on pine needles in back of the shelter where there were plenty of tent sites. This early in the season, we were not running into very many hikers, so we enjoyed their company. They also shared much information about the trails ahead of us.

Halfway into the next day's hike, we summited Warner Hill. There were large smooth rocks to sit on, a nice breeze, and a

360-degree view. A perfect place to relax and fuel up with some trail mix and cliff bars. We also were respectfully admiring Mount Greylock in the far distance, knowing we would be summiting it in a couple of days. After a refreshing 30-minute break, we were back on the trail. We hiked into Dalton at 2:00 p.m. and registered at the Shamrock Inn.

We spent some time that afternoon in the coffee shop next door that also made some great sandwiches. That evening we went around the corner to Jacob's Pub. It was packed with people on a Friday night. As we walked in, the owner started yelling several times, "Hikers in the house." He came over with a hiker logbook for us to sign, and he mentioned he had seen so many hikers come into his place to eat that he could recognize them immediately. My prime rib and Doc's haddock dinner were exceptional. We were well fueled up for the next day's 12-mile hike.

Our hike to Cheshire, another town to hike through, started at daybreak. During the hike, Doc and I had to backtrack several hundred yards. I was searching for my glasses, and Doc, at a different place, was searching for his wallet. Luckily we were both relieved to find them. This happens when 70-year-olds hike the AT.

We met a young, strong thru-hiker that day heading southbound. Turk started hiking northbound in February in Georgia. A few days ago, he had to come home to Massachusetts because of a death in the family. He could not find anyone to drive him back to Virginia, so he decided to start hiking southbound from his home state. He was a very pleasant young man enjoying his hike. We traded some information about the trail and were on our way.

During the hike to Cheshire, we encountered some thunder and rain. The highlight of the hike was reaching the Cobbles. There, at 1800 feet, we had a great view of Mount Greylock. It is Massachusetts' largest peak, and we would be tackling it the next day.

My daughter, Mori, reminded me on the phone to keep treating my side where the tick had burrowed into me several days ago in Salisbury. I decided to pick the scab off and treat it with some antibiotic ointment. After a few minutes of digging, the scab would not come off. I then realized that the gal who had yanked the tick off me a week ago had indeed failed to extract the head of the tick. The head was now part of the scab. Doc got his tweezers out and started operating on me. The pain was excruciating as he pierced the tweezers into my side and finally was able to extract the scab and the little monster's head. I cleaned the wound, packed it with Neosporin ointment, and bandaged it up.

The next day we started our climb up Greylock at 7:30 a.m. The long climb had some steep sections, with an occasional long plateau. This helped the climb immensely. We went through some enchanting thick fir tree forests on the way up. The fog was thick, which made for a welcoming cooler climb. After seven miles, we finally reached the summit and took a much-needed half-hour break. In addition, Doc took a power nap. After leaving the summit, the sun came out as we carefully descended some steep terrain. Next was a very steep 2000-foot descent, that is especially hard on 70-year-old knees and ankles. We finally arrived at Route 2 in good spirits. We were staying at the Williamstown Motel resting up for the challenging mountains of Vermont.

CHAPTER 11

Vermont

**"It is not the years in your life but
the life in your years that counts."
—Adlai Stevenson**

After a day of rest in Williamstown, Doc and I left Route 2 at the
trailhead and immediately started another climb. It was a pleasant
climb, hiking next to a fast-moving mountain stream. It lasted for
a good half hour. The white blazes led us over several interesting
rock outcroppings, and we soon came to a sign, letting us know
that we were leaving Massachusetts and entering Vermont.

It started raining, so our feet were soaked when we arrived at
the Seth Warner Shelter. The forecast showed the temperature
was to drop into the 30s. After putting on dry socks, we put
our warmest clothes on as we climbed into our sleeping bags.
However, it was very difficult to slip out of the warm comfort of
our bags in the morning.

The wind had stopped, but my temperature gage showed it
was a chilly 30 degrees. We were encouraged to see blue skies
above, so once we started hiking, the sun warmed us up. We

stopped for lunch at the Congdon Shelter. Severe weather was in the forecast, so we decided to head into Bennington.

It rained the whole night at the Catamount Inn. For the next few days, freezing temperatures, high winds, and some snow were expected. We decided to stay until the 11:00 a.m. checkout and discuss our options. I was thinking of going home for a week. Going back 5000 miles to Alaska would mean I would not be coming back to the trail anytime soon. Doc decided to rent a car and visit relatives in Pittsburgh. I finally decided to endure the weather and continue hiking through the elements.

With his rental car, Doc drove me back to the trail. It was raining and after I slung my backpack on, Doc made sure my poncho was covering my total pack. I started climbing a steep grade over large rocks and roots at noon. Two miles into the climb, the ascent became gradual, but the rain and wind increased. Three miles in, the gusts became so strong that it was knocking branches off trees. The temperature dropped significantly, and the rain occasionally became hail.

I thought of Doc traveling down the road in his warm comfortable SUV. I started second-guessing my decision and began wondering if I should have gone with him. He was driving right through Upstate New York, and I had lots of family in the Finger Lakes area. But, no, I just had to get back to the trail and test my resolve.

The wind was so strong that it caused the rain and hail to come down sideways. The gusts would about blow me over. I carefully followed the white blazes. The last thing I needed was to get lost in these conditions. Finally, after four hours of frightful hiking, I started a steep climb up Glastenbury Mountain. I knew from my AT guidebook that the Goddard Shelter was near the top. My anticipation increased as I slowly trudged up through a thick fir tree forest, which finally helped protect me from the wind.

Suddenly the very large Shelter was right in front of me. I was so relieved to have arrived. These shelters on the AT can be lifesavers. Entering, I startled a hiker curled up in his sleeping bag trying to get warm. Chuck had arrived an hour earlier. He told me that his 16-mile hike he had just finished was the most miserable hike he had ever taken. I threw over a dark-chocolate bar to him on the other side of the shelter. He looked like he could have used it.

My hand and fingers were so cold that it took me five minutes to be able to unbuckle the snaps on my backpack. I stripped off all my wet clothes and quickly put on dry ones. I soon climbed into my sleeping bag. While in my bag, I eagerly ate a subway sandwich and drank a Gatorade I had hauled up from Bennington.

Chuck had hiked over 300 miles the past few weeks from Delaware Water Gap. The rain and cold the past few days had convinced him that his section hike was over. He told me that in the morning he was going to hike back the ten miles that we had just covered and hitch a ride back to his home. We were eventually snug in our sleeping bags and well sheltered from the wind and rain that pounded the building all night. Chuck left in the morning to go home.

Chuck, an artist by trade, was heading home after days of cold and rainy weather.

It was cold and still raining, so I took my time packing up. I left with my gloves, warm clothes, and rain gear on about an hour after his departure. After 36 hours of torrential rain, the trail was filled with ankle-deep water. At times I felt like a duck waddling down the trail. After a few miles, it had warmed up a bit, and I was sort of enjoying splashing through the mud and water, just like three- and four-year-olds love to do. It was impossible to get any kind of a pace going. It was just plain difficult and slow going.

This was a miserable day of hiking endless miles of flooded trails in the rain.

Eleven miles into the hike, I was hurting after two days of intense hiking. I decided to do the last five miles on an easier Blue-Blazed Trail to Stratton Mountain Shelter. Arriving at 4:00 p.m., I was the only one there. The shelter was well kept and one of the largest on the AT. There were eight bunk beds. I chose one and laid out my pad and sleeping bag. I then opened up the other half of my Subway Italian sub and washed it down with a ginger ale. I had been thinking about this little meal all day. I was so tired that I crawled into my sleeping bag at 6:00 p.m.

As I lay there, I was trying to think of some advantages of hiking in the cold 40-degree rain, wind, and a trail filled with ankle-deep water. I started realizing that there had been no mosquitos, black flies, or snakes and that all my rainwear helped protect me against ticks. I didn't have to carry water because there was a good flowing mountain stream every 100 yards. I didn't sweat and smell as bad as usual. Not sweating so much and breathing in all the water vapor, I didn't have to stop for water so often. I almost convinced myself that these miserable conditions that I had just been through were not as bad as they seemed.

Soon after, I heard a hiker coming in. Her name was Silver Girl. She was a thru-hiker who had left Georgia in February. This five-foot 23-year-old had hiked 25 miles that day. She had graduated the previous year from college with a degree in English. Her boyfriend had hiked the first 700 miles with her and was a former thru-hiker himself. After our introductions, I was too tired to talk and soon feel asleep.

I woke at 6:00 a.m., and Silver Girl had already left. To do 25 milers every day, she pretty much hikes 10 to 12 hours a day. It was still raining, and I had a short six-mile hike into Manchester Center, so I took my time packing up. After eating a breakfast bar and finishing off the last few ounces of Gatorade, I was on my way. With my food bag empty and no water to carry, my backpack was down to 15 pounds. Food, a coffee shop, and a nice mattress to sleep on occupied my thoughts as I hiked along a much smoother and drier trail.

With a mile to go, I ran into a day hiker going back to his car, who offered me a ride into town. He dropped me off at the outfitter store. I needed a new rain cover for my backpack, and they had one that was a perfect fit. It made me so happy. I had borrowed Doc's Zpack poncho after I had lost my cover many miles back. The Zpack poncho is super light and rain proof, but is difficult to put on in the wind.

Next was a dash to Starbucks. Sitting there was Silver Girl. She was going through a large mail drop and offered me some snacks. Her sister had sent her more than she needed. After ordering my hot delicious vanilla caramel latte, we sat and visited. Hikers are always anxious to talk to one another, especially after having done the same trail for the past 1650 miles. The coffee encouraged the chatter as well. Silver Girl was going to have pizza in about an hour before she hit the trail and invited me to join her. After all the trail food she gave me, I told her the pizza was my treat.

After pizza, she put on her pack, crossed the street, and hitched a ride back to the trail. One tough gal. I went back to the coffee shop and called the Green Mountain House Hostel and found out they were not yet open for the season. I then called Sutton's place, and he was booked. Next, I called the Palmer House, which was also close by. Since I was staying for three nights, they gave me a great deal that included a continental breakfast each morning.

The zero day allowed me time to do my laundry. The next day I played nine holes of golf at the Palmer House par-three golf course, which was free for their guests. I spent more time in the coffee shop and did not miss hiking in the mountains during these freezing temperatures.

Doc returned Tuesday evening, and we went down the street in Manchester Center and had a great meal at Cilantros. The next morning we went back downtown and climbed up a flight of stairs to a restaurant called "Up For Breakfast." We then went back to the Palmer House, packed up, and checked out at 11:00 a.m. on May 10.

There are shuttle drivers available throughout the 2180 miles of the AT. Most charge $1 per mile. Some charge more, and others only charge cost of gas. Every once in a while, someone refuses any payment at all. Before Doc and I hitched a ride back to the trail from Manchester Center, we decided to stop at Starbucks for one last coffee. As we entered with our backpacks, we heard two ladies proclaim, "Hikers."

We immediately went over and easily struck up a conversation with them. They wanted to know where we were from and where were we headed. Betsy had a son who had done a thru-hike a few years ago and insisted on giving us a ride back to the trail. After about 30 minutes of fun conversation, we loaded up our backpacks into her car.

After Betsy dropped us off, we climbed up and summited Styles Peak at 3400 feet. It was cold, and we encountered an inch of new snow for about a mile between Styles Peak and Peru Peak.

We finally arrived at the Peru Peak Shelter and decided to build a campfire to warm up. Doc also boiled some water for hot chocolate that helped us wash down our sub sandwiches.

I was careful, maneuvering over slippery planks at 3500 feet in Vermont.

The previous year I did about 1200 miles of the AT. Every day since then, I have experienced sciatica. I probably did too many 20 milers last year, and the backpack caused a lot of jolting on my lower back. I was now doing fewer miles per day, but the jolting continued. I often massaged my backside and did stretches that my health-care provider gave me to do. I needed to do more slack-packing to lighten my load.

Doc and I took our time packing up and even took time to boil water for hot oatmeal before hitting the trail. We stopped every two miles for lengthy snack breaks on this hike. When we arrived at Little Rock Pond (mile 1670), we were amazed at the beauty of the little lake and the surrounding area. The shelter was large and rather new looking, but there were lots of flat area covered with pine needles, so we decided to take advantage of the nice weather and set up our tents. Hiking or camping on pine needles was very soothing for me. The scent also enhanced the experience. I have been surprised to find pine forests throughout Connecticut, Massachusetts, and Vermont. We had a nice campfire and thoroughly enjoyed the evening.

After a good night's sleep, Doc and I packed up and left our campsite at Little Rock Pond at 5:30 a.m. The plan was to board a city bus at Vermont Route 103. The bus would take us to its main bus station in Rutland. This bus station was right next to the Yellow Deli hostel. Six miles into the hike, we came to Bully Brook. The water was cascading wildly, and we spent 15 minutes trying to find a safe spot to cross. Finally, off came our socks and shoes, and we managed to cross without falling in. This put us behind schedule.

Our pace picked up, knowing if we were not at the bus stop in time, the next bus would not come for four hours. We finally arrived with only five minutes to spare. The bus ride into Rutland was most enjoyable. We checked in at the hostel, showered, and then enjoyed an excellent meal at their very impressive restaurant.

The next day, our shuttle driver picked us up and delivered us back to the trail at daybreak. Since we would end up back at the same hostel for the night, we left most of our gear there. Our packs only weighed about five pounds for this difficult 15-mile hike.

Eventually we started a long steep climb to the top of Killington Mountain (about 3900 feet). There was winter snow, sometimes two and three feet deep near the top. this ridgeline with this snow, lasted for about a mile. There was also thick evergreen for several miles at the top as well. It seemed like forever reaching Route 4. Once there, we hiked a few hundred yards up the highway to Pico Resort to catch the bus back to the Yellow Deli Hostel. After showers, Doc and I walked a half block down the street and enjoyed excellent angus burgers at Kelvans restaurant.

After another restful night on a mattress, Doc and I decided to take the $1 bus from Yellow Deli hostel back to the trail and do a short four-mile hike in the rain to Mountain Meadows Lodge. We made reservations and had mail drops waiting there. A mile before arriving, we hiked through a beautifully kept Gifford Woods State Park.

When we arrived at the lodge, we found it to be as charming inside as the setting was outside. The lodge was a unique refuge on a dirt road in the woods. It was originally a barn built in 1857. The barn was first turned into a cross-country ski lodge. Several owners over the years had made upgrades. Bill, a chef and the present owner, bought the 60-bed lodge in 2006. He mostly provides a unique place for weddings and other big events. It is right on the AT and provides an incredible B&B for hikers.

The next morning, after an incredible breakfast at the lodge, Doc and I hiked up the road a half mile to a store and deli on Route 7. We had them make us subs to take with us. After returning to the lodge, we started hiking about noon. My left ankle has always been my weak ankle. It occasionally turns on the AT, but nothing serious. One mile out of the Mountain Meadows Lodge, I turned my right ankle on a small branch on the trail. I ended up limping five miles over a tough little trail to the Stony Brook Shelter. On the way, we came upon a stream with a small pool of cold water. I did not hesitate to take off my socks and shoes to soak my ankles.

Holcomb relaxing and enjoying a much needed cold ankle soak.

When we finally arrived at the shelter, the ankle had slightly swollen. I took two ibuprofen, laid down on my sleeping bag, and used my backpack to help elevate my foot. I worried about whether I would be able to hike the ten miler planned for the next day.

Having coached high school cross-country running and basketball for 20 years, I knew a bit about taping ankles. Unfortunately, the only tape I had was about a foot and a half of duct tape. I decided to make a one-strip stirrup for my right foot and then secure it with a small piece of tape around my lower shin. I told Doc that I was going to be going real slow, hoping that I would not turn the ankle again. We made oatmeal and soon hit the trail. The duct tape seemed to give the ankle some good support, and we moved along at half pace. Doc was worried about me that day and never let me out of his sight.

The highlight was climbing the ladder of the Lookout Cabin (mile 1718) and seeing spectacular 360-degree views of Vermont on a beautiful day. As we were eating our sandwiches and lying in the warm sun, a group of day hikers arrived with their guide for lunch. They were staying at a lodge several miles away and were doing a week of day hikes. They asked us many questions about long-distance hiking.

At this location, we were able to get phone reception, and I was able to connect with Penny to find everything was fine at home. After a long lunch stop there, we reluctantly decided to leave this scenic high mountaintop. Three more miles and we arrived at the Wintturi Shelter at 3:00 p.m.

At the shelter, there was another nice cold pool of water at the base of a little waterfall where I was able to soak my ankle. After Doc boiled some water, I poured it into my dehydrated dinner of hamburger and potatoes. After washing it down with plenty of ice-cold spring water from the waterfall, I took two more ibuprofen.

On Wednesday, May 17, Doc and I started hiking at daybreak. Seven miles into our hike, we decided to stop at Teago General Store in South Pomfret. We had hiked by the town's Suicide Six Downhill Ski Area and found out at the store that it was a very economical place to downhill ski. We were hiking by a ski slope every day in Vermont.

What a great breakfast at the general store. In addition, we had fresh sandwiches made to take with us. I also chugged down two 10-ounce bottles of chocolate milk and bought a cold 32-ounce bottle of Gatorade to take with me.

Back on the trail, we had some climbs, but the trail was unusually smooth. The trail designers for this section took us to many scenic lookouts at the top of the mountains. We also came to this impressive rock fence that we followed for a good mile. I have seen these rock fences at the tops of mountains almost every day since leaving Georgia. Hikers get used to seeing them, but seeing them daily is a constant reminder of the incredible labor that went in to building these in the 18th and 19th centuries. They most likely served as property lines and probably used as livestock fences as well.

It was 90 degrees out, but Doc and I enjoyed a beautiful trail along a rock wall, before entering West Hartford, Vermont.

We arrived at Thistle Hill Shelter at 2:00 p.m. and decided to hike five more miles into West Hartford. My thermometer showed 91 degrees. The heat made it quite difficult for two old guys from Alaska, so we stopped frequently for water.

My ankle seemed a bit stronger, but I was careful not to turn it again. As we walked, the trail was relatively smooth, which allowed for a quicker pace. We arrived in West Hartford and spotted a large AT sign on Linda's barn. That was her notice to hikers that she was a trail angel. Knocking on her door to ask permission to tent in her yard, she greeted us with ice-cold root beer and watermelon. It was greatly appreciated after an exhaustingly 17-mile hike in the 90-degree heat. Linda provides refreshments to hikers during the hiking season. What a generous lady.

Doc and I departed West Hartford at six the next morning after enjoying a cup of hot coffee that Linda had thoughtfully brewed for us. We immediately had a long climb up to the summit of Happy Hill. We soon stopped at a very picturesque Happy Hill Shelter to drink a liter of water out of the cold mountain stream.

Having hiked two days in a row, we were suffering from the 90-degree heat and high humidity. Every couple of miles we stopped at a mountain steam to drink and refill our water bottles. At 11:30 a.m. on Thursday, May 18, we came out of the woods at Elm Street and followed it for one mile to the very unique Norwich Inn. Our bodies needed fuel and rest, so we registered for two nights. We were giving the weather a chance to cool down as well.

After showers, we could not find a place to wash our filthy hiking clothes. They had at least ten layers of sweat from the last six days of hiking. The smell was so bad that we were surprised they even let us in the inn. It was just plain rank. Doc called Warren Thayer, who was on a list of trail angels in Norwich. He said he lived less than a mile away, could pick us up in two hours and that we could do our laundry at his place.

That evening, Doc and I went across the street to a restaurant, had dinner, and discussed our options. The White Mountains were ahead, which meant much more difficult terrain to traverse. These mountains, all through New Hampshire, reach 5000 to 6000 feet and still have lots of winter snow and ice. Severe weather through the Whites can suddenly appear, and the many huts do not open until June. On top of that, my ankle was still swollen and sore. I felt very uncomfortable about safely continuing our hike on the AT. We decided to sleep on it.

The next morning, we had breakfast at the inn and reluctantly decided that the safe thing to do was to end this section hike. We decided to take a leisurely walk across the bridge over the Connecticut River, leaving Vermont and entering Hanover, New Hampshire. We strolled by the Dartmouth campus following the white blazes down the busy college town's Main Street. We made a beeline for the front door of a gelato shop. After choosing our flavors, we sat outside enjoying the warm weather and the delicious ice cream. We reminisced about the 200 miles we had hiked and camped together.

Saturday morning we still felt that it was time to end our hike. At the 11:00 a.m. checkout, we headed for the bus station. I was excited to go home but, at the same time, disappointed about this section hike ending early.

On the express bus to the Boston airport, I hesitantly texted Penny that I was coming home. This would be the fifth time that she had received this message over the past two years. I was relieved when she seemed happy that I was on my way.

CHAPTER 12

Back to Maine

"Success is not final, failure is not fatal,
it is the courage to continue that counts."
—Winston Churchill

After three months of rest, I decided to head back to Northern Maine to finish the southern 50 miles of the 100 Mile Wilderness. It was the first of September. After departing Anchorage, I arrived 24 hours later at the Appalachian Hostel in Millinocket, Maine. The hostel was at its capacity of 35 hikers. The next day, "Old Man," the owner of the hostel, dropped me off in the middle of the 100 Mile Wilderness at Crawford Lake. That's where I was rescued by Scott Jurek's support crew two years ago.

It was a beautiful day, and the temperature was a perfect 65 degrees. It felt so good moving through the quiet of the woods. The highlight of the day was reaching the summit of White Cap Mountain. As I neared the summit, there were hundreds of large rocks carefully positioned as steps. Hikers find rock steps like this throughout the 2180 miles of the Appalachian Trail. The labor-intensive efforts involved in these engineering feats are astonishing.

I was awed by the manhours that went into meticulous setting hundreds of large rocks into steps near the summit of White Cap Mountain. This work is seen throughout the length of the Appalachian Trail, but here, the steps seemed to go on forever.

It was late afternoon, and I had another four miles of steep descent to reach the Sidney Tappan Campsite. I soon departed the summit. As it turned dark, my luck ran out. A half mile before reaching my campsite, I tripped and took a hard forward tumble, injuring my wrists, breaking both of my hiking poles and turning my right ankle in the process. I slowly stood up and tried to process what just happened. I was devastated.

Holding what was left of my hiking poles, I carefully started hobbling down the trail. Reaching the campsite, a hiker named Cash Money was cooking over a campfire. Two brothers (Huckleberry and Blacksheep) were also there in separate tents. I unpacked and set my tent up. I then took off my hiking shoes and put on my flip-flops. I needed water. Unfortunately, the water source for this campsite was down a steep 100 yard muddy rooted side trail.

I put my headlight on and moved very carefully down the Blue-Blazed Trail. When I reached the water source, I found it to be a very weak stream. With my hands, I dug an area in the stream deep enough to soak my ankle in a pool of water. After about a half hour, I filled my water bottle with the ice-cold spring water and carefully hiked back up.

Exhausted and somewhat discouraged, I climbed into my tent and slipped into my sleeping bag. I took two ibuprofen, placed my empty backpack under my sleeping bag so that my feet were elevated, and prayed that my ankle would not swell during the night. I decided to deal with the broken hiking poles in the morning.

I woke up as I heard Huckleberry and Blacksheep breaking camp. My ankle was slightly swollen. I started taping it with adhesive tape, hoping it would keep me from turning it again. I packed up and was patching up my hiking poles with duct tape as the brothers started down the trail. I left about ten minutes later and eventually caught up to them as they were taking some pictures. We leapfrogged with one another all day.

The last thing I wanted was to turn my right ankle again. The descents were steep and especially difficult to maneuver down. The tape job seemed to be helping my ankle with support. All of a sudden we were pleasantly surprised with about five miles of a much smoother trail. After crossing a wide ford, I took my pack off and waded back out barefooted to a large rock that reached above the surface. There I sat and soaked my feet and ankles for a good 20 minutes.

The brothers arrived, and we soon started another challenging climb. Once we reached the top, we descended a long steep side trail down to a campsite next to the very large Chairback Pond. My ankle seemed to especially bother me on the descents, but I was happy to get through the nine-mile trek without turning it again.

I ran into about 40 northbound hikers that day. Many of them were anxious thru-hikers ready for their 2180-mile adventure to be over. A person has to be fit and very mentally strong to accomplish the entire 2180 miles in the span of one year. I have great respect for successful thru hikers. Even moreso, there have been some northbound thru hikers who reach the summit of

When I saw this climb near the summit of Chairback Mountain, I experienced another, *'you've got to be kidding me'* moment.

Mount Kahtahdin, and do a yoyo. That means after completing the entire 2180 miles, they turn around and do the entire trail in reverse!

It had rained all night, which made my pack a little heavier the next day. Huckleberry and Blacksheep were still packing up as I started hiking. The trail was filled with water, and all the rain made the rocks and roots especially slippery. As I struggled up the rough terrain, the brothers caught up with me. I soon looked up to a steep boulder climb near the top of Chairback Mountain and wondered if I had the energy to continue.

There was no way around it, so I slowly maneuvered up through the challenging traverse in the rain. Just before reaching Chairback Mountain Shelter, I stumbled again and fell face-first into a mud puddle. I was soaked, but the hard rain soon washed the mud from me. After a few hundred yards more, I joined Huckleberry, his brother, and a few others in the shelter to dry out a bit and take a needed break.

After about 20 minutes, the brothers took off, and I followed about ten minutes later. A couple of miles up the trail, I met up with them again. They were saturated and had decided to head for the Gorman Chairback Lodge, which was only about a mile off the trail. They invited me to join them, but I foolishly turned them down.

It was getting late, and I had a couple more miles to reach a small campsite that was showing in my guidebook. Three strong hikers from Kentucky passed me. They were headed to the next shelter that was four miles ahead. The downpour made for miserable hiking conditions, especially with my weak ankle and unstable poles.

About 6:00 p.m., I finally reached the campsite that had room for only one tent. There was a nice flowing stream. I emptied the contents of my backpack and placed everything inside my pack cover to keep the gear dry. I set up my tent in the rain. I quickly put my backpack and the pack cover (with all its contents) into the tent.

It was warm out, so I stripped down to my birthday suit. I wrung out a good pint of sweat and rainwater from my hiking clothes. No food bag was hung that night. Once inside, I organized all my gear. I then ate some trail mix, cheese, and fig bars. I was exhausted. As I lay there in the comfort of my sleeping bag, I was hoping the stream next to me would not turn into a flash flood and wash me away during the night.

I woke at 6:00 a.m. to find the rain still pounding my tent. It was tempting to go back to sleep and stay in the tent till it stopped. At the same time, I realized it may rain all day. I decided I needed to get to the Wilson Valley Shelter (ten miles away), get out of this rain, and dry out. This Shelter would set me up for another doable ten-mile hike on Friday to Route 15, the end of the 100 Mile Wilderness.

I spent some time thinking about how to pack up in the downpour. I was warm and dry as I ate some granola, steak jerky, and some almonds. I finally stuffed my sleeping bag in its waterproof sac and pushed it to the bottom of my backpack.

Next into the backpack went everything else. I placed my waterproof pack cover over my backpack and moved it outside. I put my damp clothes back on and crawled out of the tent. After dismantling my tent, I shook as much water off it as I could. Stuffing the tent into its waterproof sac, I then placed it into the top of my backpack. I was off.

The first challenge was a very steep slippery two-mile climb up Barren Mountain. The trail was filled with water. Next came a challenging four-mile steep descent over slippery boulders, roots, and mud. At the bottom, I came to a frightful cascading Long Pond Creek water crossing. This high-water crossing after all the rain was scary. The three hikers from Kentucky who were also doing the 100 Mile Wilderness southbound had just finished crossing as I arrived. I thought, *Great, someone to rescue me if I fall in.*

I did not hesitate. My hiking shoes were already soaking wet, so I left them on as I carefully slipped in and started across. I moved one step at a time, using both taped-up poles to steady myself and find footing for each step. The noise of the raging water was deafening. Halfway across, the swift water was just above the top of my legs. One of my taped-up poles buckled; I lost my balance and momentarily fell to my knees, soaking myself to my neck. Luckily, I was able to regain my footing and very carefully continued across without further incident. What a relief to get across.

Just as I finished crossing, the sun came out, along with a nice warm breeze. I decided to unpack the entire contents of my backpack, hanging and spreading out my tent, sleeping bag, and all my clothes over willow bushes to dry. The three hikers from Kentucky passed me, wished me luck, and continued down the trail. It had been a very stressful six miles of very challenging terrain. I snacked, rested, and let all my gear and clothes dry out in the warm breeze for the next two hours.

After packing up, I super appreciated the sunny conditions, especially after enduring two days and nights of miserable wet conditions and treacherous trails. I was also feeling weak after four days of exhausting hikes. The next four miles, I struggled up and over another mountain and finally arrived at Wilson Valley Shelter at 5:00 p.m.

I claimed a spot in the shelter and spread out my sleeping pad and sleeping bag. I had a few electrolyte packages, so I made some needed Gatorade to drink. I then filled my water bottle with more Gatorade for the next day's hike. I needed some strength for the next day, so I ate a lot of steak jerky, almonds, granola, and a couple of protein bars.

The three Kentucky boys were cooking and had their three hammocks set up nearby. Five more hikers arrived.. Four of them elected to stay in the shelter and one decided to tent. It was comforting to be camping with many hikers for a change. There was lively conversation about the past two days of hiking in the rain. Six of the hikers were also planning to head home after they reached Monson.

This Wilson Valley Hut was a welcomed site. After the last few days of frightening high water crossings and solo hiking, the large crowd seemed very comforting to me.

Earlier that day, I ran into about eight middle-aged hikers going northbound, carrying backpacks, with their contents totaling about five pounds. They were spread out over about three miles and heading to their support van on a logging road. Their tents would be set up, and dinner would be ready for them when they arrived. As I struggled up these steep mountains and over this very challenging terrain with my 20-pound pack, I thought, *Maybe I should have signed up for this 100 Mile Wilderness tour.*

At daybreak the next, I heard a northbound hiker in the shelter stuffing his bag into its sac. I immediately sat up and did the same. We both worked quietly packing up, as the other three in the shelter were still sleeping. I took a little extra time to finish up the rest of my steak jerky, cheese, and almonds. I was anxious to get to the next challenging ford over Big Wilson Stream, which was just one mile ahead.

On the way, I met a hiker who had just crossed. Her advice was, "Be careful." This didn't help my anxiety that I was experiencing. When I arrived, it looked deep and was about 60 feet across. I left my shoes on and slowly slipped in. The bottom was covered with slippery rounded 12- to 16-inch diameter rocks.

Using my patched-up poles, I carefully and very slowly would step over one large rock at a time, finding proper footing each step. The progress was meticulous and slow. The water came to the tops of my legs, but the current was not the raging streams that I had crossed the day before. Finally I reached the other side. I noticed seven northbound hikers had been watching me cross. They had all camped there that night hoping the water level would drop.

I continued up the trail about a half mile to a much easier ford across ankle-deep water. After crossing, there was a bench next to a small camping area. I decided to take a 30-minute break. I took off and wrung out my socks, then dried out my insoles and shoes. After drying my feet, I put on my last pair of dry socks. I then snacked, filled my water bottle and was soon on my way.

I felt much stronger that day after a good night's rest and the large amount of food I had consumed at the last shelter. I climbed the next mountain up to a long stretch of ledges with some nice views. Three miles up from the Big Wilson Stream, I came to my next ford at Little Wilson Stream. I decided to take off my socks and shoes and wear my flip-flops across. The stream was swifter than Big Wilson but was only about 30 feet across. As I slipped into the water, it came up over my knees. Slowly and carefully, I maneuvered across without any incident. After crossing, there was a large campsite area with large stone benches. After drying off my feet and putting my dry socks and hiking shoes back on, I took another snack break to relax a bit.

Next was a climb up to a very picturesque Little Wilson Falls. The next six miles to Route 15 included many small ups and downs but no serious climbs. I arrived there at 3:30 p.m. and hitched a three-mile ride into Monson.

At Shaw's Hostel, I took a needed shower and washed my sweaty hiking clothes for my trip home. Shaw's Hostel arranged a 50-mile shuttle for me to the Quality Inn in Bangor. The next day I boarded a Concord bus to Boston Airport and then an Alaska Airlines 737 to Anchorage through Seattle.

My fall at the end of the first day of this 50-mile section hike was a devastating start. My ankle and wrist injuries, my flimsy hiking poles, the two days of downpour, the high-water crossings and the very difficult terrain, turned this hike into a nightmare. In fact, both of my section hikes in the 100 Mile Wilderness were nightmares. As I traveled back to Anchorage, I wondered whether it was worth the risk of ever returning.

CHAPTER 13

Back to Monson

"**Great works are performed
not by strength but by perseverance.**"
—**Samuel Johnson**

After 12 months, I had mentally recovered from my last hike. My wrists were still a little weak, so I knew I had to slow down to avoid any forward falls. I was planning on the seventh section hike of the AT to be my last. I had texted Crash in New Hampshire to let him know I was meeting a hiker named Seeker, on August 15, in Monson, Maine. Crash and I had briefly met Seeker two years ago at Double Springs Shelter just before entering Damascus, Virginia. I had found out that Seeker was also hiking to Hanover, New Hampshire, to complete his three-year mission of hiking the AT.

Crash answered and notified me that after I flew into Boston on August 14, he would pick me up and drive me the four hours to Monson. Not only that, I was elated that he wanted to hike the first three days to Caratunk with us.

Seeing each other for the first time in two years, there were big smiles and a hearty embrace. We headed across the parking lot to his convertible mini cooper. Crash got his name from all the car accidents he had as a teenager. He loved cars and their potential speed. As the long drive progressed, I was glad to see that over the years he had become a much safer driver.

Once we arrived at Shaw's Hiker Hostel, we found Seeker, who was resting, having just completed Mount Katahdin and the 100 Mile Wilderness. He had hiked into Monson the day before on the 13th and was taking a much-needed zero day. We were all relieved that we were on schedule to start hiking the next day as planned.

Shaw's Hostel serves an all-you-can-eat breakfast to 30 to 40 hikers every morning during the hiking season. This hostel is very organized and a comfortable place to spend the night. At a restaurant up the street, we enjoyed reminiscing over dinner that night. After a good night's sleep and an incredible breakfast, we were ready to hit the trail.

We were doing a slack pack for our first day of hiking. Our shuttle driver took us southbound out on some back roads for a 13-mile northbound hike back to Shaw's. That meant another good night's sleep and a lot more great grub. This hike was easier, not only because of our light packs but also the trail was much smoother. Half the day's hike was along a pleasant-sounding cascading stream. The other half we experienced a little rain; however, it provided some cooling from the 80-degree heat.

Our second day out, we were blessed with another beautiful day. During our 12-mile hike, the only real

I very much enjoyed this beautiful trail, slack packing back to Monson, Maine.

challenge was a steep climb up Moxie Bald Mountain. Reaching the summit at 2500 feet, we were rewarded with 360 degree views of the valleys and surrounding mountains for more than 100 miles. After a long lunch break, we had an easy, long gradual descent to our campsite, where we set up our tents for the night. We only had four water crossings the past two days. It had been a rather dry summer, so we easily waded across them.

As we hiked southbound that day, we met several thru-hikers each day heading north, anxious to finish their AT hike. Each one had a story to tell, but most of the time, there is only a pause to acknowledge one another as we pass in opposite directions. Every once in a while at evening camp, we get to visit with other hikers around a campfire.

Many hikers do the Appalachian Trail for many reasons. Some reexamine their direction in life, some hike for the camaraderie of meeting others who like to hike, and most all hikers just like getting away from their routines in life and enjoy the contrast of being out in the quietness of the forest. Others hike just for the challenge that the AT abundantly provides—the satisfaction of "I did it," whether it's a day hiker climbing a mountain on a <u>Sunday afternoon</u> or a section hiker after years of trying to finish, or a thru-hiker after six months on the trail.

Hiking in New York last year, I met this 65-year-old hiker going southbound. We stopped and chatted. He told me he had spent 20 years section hiking, trying to finish the Appalachian Trail and only had five miles to go. Having hiked over 1400 miles at the time, I sensed the incredible feeling he must be experiencing. Hikers really respect one another knowing they also endured the never-ending rugged terrain that the AT throws at you. I firmly shook his hand and warmly congratulated him as we departed.

Leaving our campsite the next morning, we had some very challenging and rugged climbs up to Pleasant Pond Mountain. The relentless trail was slow going and definitely welcoming me back to the AT. There were some positives; no bugs, it was a beautiful day, and the last six miles of the 12-mile hike were a little easier.

We had reservations at the Caratunk House. Seeker and I had taken several breaks, so Crash had arrived two hours before us. He thought one of us had been injured and was about to send search-and-rescue out to find us. That night, the hostel gave us a free shuttle five miles up the road to a rafting lodge for a farewell dinner for Crash.

It poured all night. It was nice being warm and dry. The capacity at the Caratunk House is for only nine guests. They have a great hiker supply, and most hikers on the AT need to resupply there. Paul (the owner) and his staff serve very popular milkshakes all day long to any hiker who may stop for a break. For their overnight guests, they serve an incredible breakfast. After breakfast, Seeker and I said our good-byes to Crash. The driver was ready to shuttle him back to his car, which was at Shaw's Hostel in Monson. Later that day, Crash would be driving back to his home in Southern New Hampshire.

The canoe ferry service that the AT provides for crossing the Kennebec River was free and available starting at 9:00 a.m. Seeker and I packed up and hiked a few hundred yards to the river. Arriving at 8:45 a.m., we were first in line. The planned hike was a 14 miler to West Carry Pond Shelter. After crossing, we found the first four miles to be many small ups and downs that paralleled cascading streams. We stopped at the Pierce Pond Shelter for a snack break and to fill our water bottles.

The hike had a few easy water crossings, but the last three miles was a slog through mud, rocks, and roots. After arriving, Seeker elected to sleep in the three-sided shelter. There were some nice tent spots under the large pine trees, so I elected to sleep in my well-vented tent for the night.

I felt very cautious and a little nervous, moving very slowly across this very slippery log.

There were many of these untrustworthy brook crossings that were eagerly waiting for me to slip and fall in.

Four months ago, I was diagnosed with frozen shoulders. My doctor scheduled eight weeks of physical therapy. During that time, Kelsey, my therapist, brought me back to 70 percent normal. The past six days, the physical demands of the AT trail had been really testing my shoulders durability. As Seeker and I studied the difficult terrain ahead of us from our AT maps, we decided to hike easier trails for two days to get to Route 27. We hoped this would help to ease the pounding our aging bodies were taking.

We left the West Carry Pond Shelter on August 19 at 6:00 a.m. After three miles, we took a left turn onto the Main Hut Trail and departed the AT. It was an easier trail and therefore much more enjoyable. We continued hiking eight miles on this trail and arrived at their Poplar Hut at 1:00 p.m. After showers, we were served a hearty lunch.

This fairly new multiuse Main Hut Trail System goes for 80 miles with four different huts that have capacities for over 40 guests each. The Main Hut Trail is open year-round for hikers, trail bikes, snow machines, cross-country skiers, and snowshoe hikers. They serve incredible breakfasts, lunches, and dinners, all included in the price of the night's lodging. The huts also have many other snacks and a wide variety of beverages for sale.

Seeker and I had a large two-bunk room to ourselves. There were only five other guests for the night: three ladies on a three-day hike and a father and son biking from hut to hut. For dinner, the two-person staff first served us soup and a large salad with homemade bread. Next came an all-you-can-eat spaghetti and meatball dinner. Chocolate cake was served for dessert, and there was a tour of the solar panel–powered facility that evening.

The next morning, we were served oatmeal, scrambled eggs, bacon, orange juice, and coffee. After breakfast, we were given a sack lunch to take with us. We left this luxurious oasis well rested and much better nourished. We continued southbound for three more miles on the Main Hut Trail to the Narrow Gage Pathway. This nicely groomed trail follows an old railroad bed with many picnic tables along the way. For seven more miles, this enjoyable hike was enhanced by a cascading stream next to the trail. At the end of this pathway was the Hostel of Maine on Route 27. What a beautiful bed and breakfast. There was a very large and luxurious lounge area. We stayed in one of their bunkrooms for $40, which was a great bargain that included breakfast.

The next day, we followed Carabou Pond Road for seven miles that eventually took us back to the AT. The most difficult climb was near the end of our hike, up to the summit of Popular Ridge. Rain was in the forecast, so after another mile, we decided to spend the night in the Popular Ridge Shelter.

The next morning, it was raining as we immediately started a very long steep climb up Saddleback Junior Mountain. It was more

than a junior. I mentioned to Seeker, "If this was junior, what would senior be like." We eventually reached the top; what we had gained in elevation, we were soon to lose, as we carefully descended boulder after boulder, for it seemed like forever. After two hours of hiking, we met eight separate hikers going northbound who had camped at Redington Campsite. After reaching the large camping area, we stopped for a snack and filled our water bottles for the hike ahead. We put our rain gear on, as the drizzle had turned to a downpour.

Next was a long steep climb up more very slippery rocks and boulders. We had to use our hands to get up many

Climbing Saddleback Mountain in the rain was more than a struggle.

of these steep grades. It was slow going up to the summit of this next mountain called The Horn. We were now in the fog above tree line, totally exposed to the cold, high winds and dangerous hypothermic conditions. I could barely see Seeker, who was only about 50 feet in front of me.

Our pace was brisk, but we were careful as we hiked up to and over the summit of Saddleback Senior. The sleet was hitting us hard from a howling crosswind. Above tree line for a good three miles, we were relieved when we finally descended through thick evergreen trees. This gave us much relief from the cold wind. The trail going down Saddleback Senior was very steep. We meticulously picked and slid our way down over 2000 feet for the next two hours. To add to the challenge, the water from the rain was roaring down the trail. The roots and rocks on the way down were super slippery.

After eight hours of this exhausting nine-mile hike, we finally reached the Piazza Shelter. It was a welcome site and felt good to get out of the rain. We were starving after losing an incredible amount of calories over the eight-hour slog. We took our packs off and gobbled down all of our last snacks. I consider this hike to have been one of the most exhausting and challenging of my life.

Finally reaching Route 4, we hitched a ride into Rangeley and especially enjoyed hot showers at the Town & Lake Motel. The motel was near many eating establishments. The Red Onion served a wide variety of lunches. Across the street from the Red Onion was a restaurant called the Park and Main. We thoroughly enjoyed two excellent evening meals there.

Rangeley is a neat little town. After eight days of hiking, we decided to take a zero day to rest and fuel up there. I missed my wife every day on the trail. As I drank her favorite vanilla-caramel latte at a coffee shop in this quaint little town, I lifted my cup to a very generous craft talented gal, who I love very much. It was August 23, our 43rd anniversary. I was glad she was spending a few days with many of our grandkids whom she loves dearly. It was hard for this married hiker to keep hiking the trail, when I had so many loved ones back home, especially being 5000 miles away. I called her this morning to wish her an enjoyable day.

The Appalachian Trail in Maine is sometimes brutal. Seeker and I decided to do a 13-mile slack pack between Route 4 and Route 17, which would allow us another night in Rangeley. Our light packs helped us hike over many challenging knolls, mud holes, and large step downs. Everyday my 73-year-old joints took a pounding.

A lanky trail runner went zooming by us in running shorts on this 13-mile hike. At the end of the hike, when we arrived at the parking lot trailhead, we found out that it was Karel Sabbe, a Belgian runner trying to break the AT speed record. He was averaging 51 miles a day. Karel also had the current speed record for the 2700 mile Pacific Crest Trail. Karel had departed northbound an hour before we arrived. After we signed some paperwork verifying he had passed us during this section, his pit crew offered us a nine-mile ride back to Rangeley. The next week, we found out that he did break the record.

The next day after our 13-mile slack pack, Seeker and I decided to sleep in a bit till checkout. We went for breakfast and had arranged a shuttle back to the trail at 11:00 a.m. We had really enjoyed Rangeley. The Town & Lake Motel was in a scenic location, had reasonable rates, and was close to everything in town. In addition, a fine outfitter store was nearby that provided shuttles. It was a unique and hiker friendly place. In the winter, it was a popular downhill ski area.

The next day we paid our shuttle driver $25 for the 25-mile ride back to the trail. Arriving at the trailhead on Route 17, I realized I did not have my phone. It had hundreds of AT pictures, along with many of my journals of the AT. I was not hiking until I found that phone. After checking everywhere in the truck, I requested the driver to take me back to the motel. He said he would, but the extra 50-mile round trip would cost me another $25. Seeker headed on up the trail. My anxiety level had skyrocketed during the 30-minute drive back. As we drove into the parking lot of the motel, there on the arm of a lounge chair, where we had waited for the shuttle, was my phone.

Seeker was a good hour ahead of me when the driver dropped me off at the trailhead. I took my time, as Seeker and I had only planned a five miler up to the Bemis Mountain Shelter. After the first mile, I came across trail magic. Thank you, Gregg and Geri. I stopped to rest and enjoyed a cold ginger ale in the 80-degree heat before the four-mile climb up to the shelter. Arriving at the shelter, Seeker was already settled in.

The next day, the 80-degree heat and high humidity continued to make the hike much more difficult for us. After five hours of hiking, we eventually started a steep climb up to the summit of Old Blue Mountain. There were several northbound thru-hikers resting at the top. We took a 30-minute lunch break and enjoyed a pleasant breeze.

At noon we started a very steep 2000-foot drop that took us over two hours. It

Descending Old Blue Mountain was tedious, tiring and took much patience.

was nerve racking and dangerous. We went especially slow to avoid any injury.

We finally reached South Arm Road and hitched a nine-mile ride into Andover, where we had reservations at the Pine Ellis Hostel. I drank a lot of water that day in the 80-degree heat, but it never seemed to quench my thirst. After two large thick milkshakes and three 20-ounce sodas at the local general store, I finally felt hydrated.

Seeker and I, after hiking 230 miles of Maine trails, decided to skip the most dangerous Mahoosuc Arm and Mahoosuc Notch. At our age, we did not feel it was wise to risk permanent injury. You may view videos of these sections online.

After a good night's sleep at the Pine Ellis Hostel, Seeker and I shuttled 25 miles from Andover to Gorham to prepare for hiking the AT in New Hampshire. As our shuttle driver zipped around the curvy mountain roads at 65 mph, I reached up and grabbed the handle located above the window with both my hands. At these speeds, my foot would press hard to the floor as she caught other vehicles, slam on her brakes, and tailgate within two car lengths. I would feel a little whiplash as she would put the car in overdrive to eventually pass these cars.

There were three different areas where road construction only allowed one-way traffic. To her, *slow* meant 50 mph through these zones. I was wondering if the dangerous hiking section we were skipping would have been safer than this terrifying ride. When we arrived at the Rattle River Hostel, my knuckles were white. We decided to take another zero to rest up for the next difficult section.

A funny thing happened at the hostel. As I was chatting with this gal who looked familiar, she asked me my trail name. When I told her Holcomb, she said, "I thought I recognized you." The previous year near Falls Village, Connecticut, she was hiking southbound as I was hiking northbound, and we had stopped and chatted for about 15 minutes before going our separate ways. I had done a journal piece on her earlier in chapter 10. Crazy coincidence.

This year, Charmin was hiking with a gal with a car. They would drive to a hostel, then have the hostel drive them back 20 or 30 miles to a trailhead. They would then do a two or three day hike back to the hostel and their car. They would then drive to the next hostel and continue this pattern with the convenience of having a car to explore the area around the Appalachian Trail. It was another unique way to hike the AT.

By now Seeker and I had completed 2000 miles of the AT. We were beginning to feel like this was enough of an accomplishment. Any more miles, we were considering extra credit. Next we were planning a difficult three-day hike to Pinkham Notch. After two days of rest at the Rattle River Hostel, we were headed for the Imp Shelter, eight miles away. The terrain was steep and difficult, especially up and over the 4000-foot Mount Moriah. The temperature was 90 degrees, and the high humidity made the climbs much more exhausting. The eight-mile hike took us eight hours. The highlight of the day were some spectacular views of the White Mountains of New Hampshire.

Mount Moriah was steep and slow going, but after two days of rest, we excelled.

This climb up North Carter Mountain in the rain was just plain dangerous for this 74 year old hiker. This treacherous climb, led me to believe, that I had experienced enough of the AT.

The day marked 13 days for me without a fall, and that breaks my record. We decided to get an early start the next day due to the very challenging trail. A mile into the hike, we came to an incredibly steep, dangerous boulder climb up North Carter Mountain. To add to the challenge, it started raining, and the wind started howling. The steep, wet, slippery boulder-climbing was very scary at times, especially with our 20-pound packs on our backs. In addition, we were each carrying an extra five pounds of water, since there were no water sources for this route. The climbs were tedious and nerve racking. There were a couple of more climbs up to Carter Dome at 5000 feet.

I was wearing a hat that displayed "ALASKA" on the front. As I was hiking southbound on this hike, a thru-hiker named Pocket, going northbound, stopped and asked me if I was from Anchorage. I said yes, and she said, "So am I." Pocket continued to exclaim, "These AT trails are ridiculous." We both agreed that the trail designers had gone too far, many times cutting the trail over very dangerous terrain. She was near the end of her thru-hike and was obviously ready for it to be over. We wished each other safe hiking and went our separate ways.

The last mile took us down a steep dangerous 1500-foot drop that took us an hour to descend. We were tired but so relieved to arrive at the Carter Hut without an injury. We checked in at 2:00 p.m. and immediately were served some delicious potato soup and coffee cake. We went to our bunkhouse and unpacked, cleaned up a bit and then collapsed on our bunks for a much-needed rest.

This hut had a capacity for 40 guests, but there were only 6 of us there for the night. Three of the guests were nurses from New York City, who had just graduated from nursing school. They were doing some day hikes in the White Mountains. The all-you-can-eat dinner was served at 6:00 p.m. First came some delicious tomato soup with fresh warm homemade bread. The next course was an excellent salad. The third course was a delicious pasta dinner with cooked peas as a side. For dessert, peach pie and coffee. The three-person staff waited on us nonstop and provided us some after-dinner entertainment as well. Everyone was in a festive mood, and it was an enjoyable ending after a tough day of hiking.

There are several of these AMC (Appalachian Mountain Club) huts and lodges on the AT throughout the White Mountains of New Hampshire. They have large capacities and are strategically placed about eight miles apart. In the White Mountains, severe weather conditions can occur without much warning. Thunderstorms are especially dangerous because much of the trail in the Whites is above tree line.

My shoulders would always ache after a day's hike. A couple of ibuprofen in the evening would help the discomfort for about eight hours. I did my arm and shoulder stretch exercises, but the rugged trail of the Appalachian Trail demanded a lot from them. I was worried that I was doing them permanent damage.

After a great night's sleep at the Carter Notch Hut and a breakfast of oatmeal, scrambled eggs, bacon, and pancakes, Seeker and I were ready to hike. We immediately started a steep 1200-foot climb up Wildcat Mountain A. After descending a bit, the next climb was up Wildcat Mountain C. I do not recall that there was a Wildcat B. The final steep climb was up Wildcat Mountain D. There at the top was a large elevated deck with incredible views of Mount Washington and the Presidential Range. About a hundred feet below the observation deck, a gondola was loudly calling our names. To avoid killing ourselves hiking 2000 feet down another notorious steep, dangerous trail, we did not hesitate to pay the $7.50 for a very enjoyable ride down.

It was breathtaking, reaching the top of Wildcat Mountain D and witnessing for the first time, an incredible view of the very majestic Mount Washington.

At the bottom, Seeker and I enjoyed an excellent lunch at the ski resort restaurant. We then hiked up the road a mile to Joe Dodge Lodge. At this large AMC Lodge, we enjoyed an all-you-can-eat buffet dinner, a restful night's sleep, and a great buffet breakfast, all included in the price for the night's lodging.

The next day we decided to hire the tour van to drive us up to the top of Mount Washington. I refused to look down, as the tour van maneuvered around the narrow steep curvy road to the 6000-foot summit. The tour driver informed us that some of the motorcyclists who reach the top have to hire drivers to drive their bikes back down. It is that scary. It was chilly, and there was thick fog at the top. To warm up, we stopped for some hot chocolate and a sandwich at the large visitor's center. Soon we departed. The immediate descent was steep, and the trail was covered with large rocks everywhere. We were soon passed by Austen, a worker at the Lake of the

Halfway to the Lake of the Clouds Hut, I was startled and impressed when Austen zipped by me, gracefully moving over the rugged trail with her 85 pound pack of supplies.

Clouds Hut, carrying an 85-pound pack of supplies from the visitor's center. We were amazed at her agility to move over the rocks so smoothly.

The Lake of the Clouds Hut was a little more than a mile down from the top of Mount Washington. It is the largest hut in the White Mountains with a lodging capacity for 90 guests. All the food and supplies are hiked down and all the garbage hiked up to the Mount Washington Visitor Center, every day by the workers.

Lake of the Clouds Hut.

Arriving at the Lake of the Clouds Hut, we took a 20-minute break. The fog had lifted, and the visibility was endless. Being Labor Day weekend, hikers were everywhere. The hut was busy with hikers snacking and visiting at the tables. After checking out the hut, we found ourselves hiking on this high ridgeline walk for several miles to the Mizpah Hut. The 70-degree temperature made for the hiking conditions very enjoyable. This hike was one of the most pleasant hikes I have ever had. The views were spectacular in every direction. Seeker and I were in awe of the vistas all around us and kept stopping to take it all in. I kept thinking that this hike would be an appropriate ending of this three-year AT adventure of mine.

With incredible views of mountaintops in every direction, it was exhilarating, hiking along this ridgeline between the Lake of the Clouds Hut to the Mizpah Hut.

It was a steep descent to the Mizpah Hut. It was near capacity, and Seeker elected to stay in the hut. I was able to get one of the remaining tent sites for $5, which meant I would be eating from my food pack rather than the all-you-can-eat meals for the guests.

The next morning I started the day with some Jim Croce, the Beatles, and the Mamas and Papas on my iPod. I was feeling pretty good after the previous day's hike and a good night's sleep in my tent. After Seeker finished his all-you-can-eat breakfast in the hut dining room, we hit the trail at 8:00 a.m. We had a gradual five-mile hike down the Crawford Path along another cascading stream.

In 1819, the historic Crawford Path was first cleared by Abel Crawford and his son, Ethan. The Crawfords guided many groups to the summit of Mount Washington. The trail was improved to a bridle path to Mount Washington from 1840 to 1870. In 1870, it became a path for hiking only. Most day hikers use this more gradual ascent to the ridgeline that we had hiked down the day before. The two hours it took us to come down, we met over 100 day hikers on their way up. It was another enjoyable hike.

We had reservations at the AMC Highland Center, a large lodge for hikers. It was a relaxing day. We enjoyed a nice lunch and an all-you-can-eat barbecue buffet dinner. Seeker and I felt very satisfied with the previous day's ridge walk we experienced from the top of Mount Washington to the Mizpah Hut. We decided to again skip more dangerous areas of the AT. We hired a shuttle driver to take us to the base of Mount Cube for a three-day march to our finish line in Hanover, New Hampshire.

It was another hot and humid day, which made the climb up Mount Cube very difficult. The humidity was so high that the many rocks and boulders were sweating in the shade. At the top, I could have easily filled a pint jar with the sweat I wrung out of my shirt and hat. After the long climb, we were, however, rewarded at the summit at 3000 feet, with a nice breeze and incredible views. We lounged in the open breeze for over an hour, eating a deli sandwich, drinking a sports drink, and munching on fig bars for dessert. Many northbound

Along the entire length of the Appalachian Trail, thousands of volunteers help to maintain the trail. Plank walk construction is one example and they really help to preserve the trail. It requires an incredible amount of hard labor. Many times these monster planks have to be hand carried up to the top of mountains.

hikers were there snacking, enjoying the views, and resting from their exhausting climbs.

Reluctantly to leave the cooling breeze, we threw our backpacks on and started our descent in the 90-degree heat. The humidity was brutal. The rocks and boulders that were sweating in the shade made the descent very slippery. It was a very slow process finding foot placements.

Halfway down the mountain, we came to a cool mountain stream. There were eight northbound hikers resting in the shade and quenching their thirst at this very welcomed oasis. We filled our water bottles and took a Blue-Blazed side trail 400 yards straight up from the AT to the very large Hexacuba Shelter. We laid out our sleeping pads and sleeping bags, and our tired and overheated bodies collapsed for a needed rest.

Seeker and I left the next morning with our headlamps on. We were hoping the cool morning temperature would make the hike more bearable. After an hour descent to South Jacobs Brook, we took our first snack and water break. We eventually filled our water bottles for the four-mile climb up Smarts Mountain.

We came to this road where a huge pile of these planks (eight feet long and four inches thick) had been unloaded. As we climbed, we noticed trail crews had been hand carrying these monsters up to near the top of Smarts Mountain. The plank walks help hikers over muddy and bog areas. Through the 100 Mile Wilderness, some of these plank walks are over 100 yards long.

I also noticed crews had carried and buried long logs along this trail to divert rain water away from the trail. This tremendously helps prevent trail erosion. All along the Appalachian Trail, hikers notice and appreciate these engineering feats and hard work that help to preserve the trail. Take notice, Vermont.

Trail maintenance on the Appalachian Trail is helped through grants and donations. Hiking clubs and individual volunteers are constantly helping to improve the trail and shelters. Many times former thru-hikers come back and volunteer at different sections. Many hikers also help to move branches out of the way as they hike. They also help to keep the hundreds of shelters clean as they pass through. We rested at the top of Smarts Mountain at 3200 feet for a good 30 minutes. There was a fire tower that provided incredible 360-degree views. There were campsites and a large shelter at the summit where fire wardens overnighted many years ago.

Soon we began our steep descent. My streak of 17 days without falling ended today. I slipped on a large wet boulder face, my feet went out from under me, and I landed on my butt. Plenty of padding there, so the only damage was to my ego. Our 12-mile hike ended at the very nice Lyme Inn in Lyme, New Hampshire. We enjoyed a great meal across the street.

The next day as we hiked toward Hanover, Seeker and I reflected about our AT journey that had taken us three years to complete. We reminisced and, at the same time, tried to comprehend all that we were feeling. We were happy that the grueling ordeal of the difficult climbs and dangerous descents would be no more. We felt blessed to have avoided serious injury. On the other hand, there was a sadness of leaving the vistas, the quietness of hiking in the woods and the camaraderie with other hikers along the trail.

We came to a nice place to sit and enjoyed some sandwich wraps that we had bought the night before at a deli in Lyme. We talked about the transitions we were about to make from the routines of hiking all day, to the routines of daily life back home. Seeker asked me, "What's next?" I responded, "Smoother walks on the golf course."

As we threw our backpacks on for the last time, we slowed our pace and took some pictures of some old stone fences that had been standing there for hundreds of years.

As we came close to Hanover, the trail zigzagged around these monster boulders covered with bright-green moss known as the Velvet Rocks. The easier trail that day took us through a lot of pine forest, with the trail covered in pine needles. Pine forests always seem to make the hike a little more enjoyable.

I was in awe of the amount of time and work that was done by early Americans, hand carrying and assembling these rock walls that are still standing today.

The temperature was 90 degrees as we came out of the woods. We found ourselves hiking alongside some of the Dartmouth athletic fields. The white blazes led us along streets to the unique college downtown area. It was lunchtime, and we soon joined many patrons at a popular restaurant. We luckily found two barstools at the end of the long counter.

Seeker ordered a large milkshake and I ordered a large root beer float. The air-condition space seemed like heaven to our overheated and smelly bodies. We clicked glasses, congratulated one another, and took our time quenching our thirst with the ice-cream drinks. We eventually found our way to our hotel. After showers, we celebrated with wine and a steak dinner. The next day we boarded the Dartmouth Coach to the Boston airport to fly home.

This three-year journey sent me from Alaska, back to the Appalachian Trail seven times. I took 20 days of rest out of the

170 days on the trail. There was a whole lot of climbing and descending mountains for over 2000 miles. I did take a few shortcuts, but 95 percent of the time I followed the white blazes of the Appalachian Trail. I met some wonderful people. There were many who gave me refreshments and rides to and from the trail. There were others who just wanted to converse about what hiking the AT was like. The hundreds of hikers I met were very pleasant and considerate people. The social life on the AT is very special, unique and treasured by most hikers. Many section and thru hikers continue to communicate and plan reunions for many years after the hike.

It was peaceful, hiking in the quiet of the woods, totally removed from the hectic traffic of the city and all the political drama and bias that we are bombarded with by today's media. As I hiked, I enjoyed the hours and hours of alone time. Time seemed to slip by quickly, especially when I found myself in deep thought. I spent a lot of time reflecting on my life and what a precious gift it has been. I dwelled on the memories I have received as a schoolteacher, coach, husband, parent, and grandparent.

There were times I loved being on the trail, but hiking in the cold pelting rain was not one of them. During those times, I would desperately ask myself, "What on earth am I doing out here?" There were other times when the terrain made the hiking just plain tough going and difficult to endure. During some of those times, I reminded myself that it's the things we work for that brings lasting satisfaction. This helped me to keep going. Hiking over hundreds of mountains, along their ridgelines, through the trees, and by the cascading streams, was an incredible adventure. The people I met, the variety of terrain I hiked and all the experiences I had on the trail, became a part of me, forever.

Some Enjoyable Appalachian Trail Northbound Shorts

(The National Geographic Map Books of the AT help at showing shortcuts)

I took seven of the following shortcuts (*). If I would have known about the others, I would have taken them as well. I did see many thru-hikers taking the shortcuts that I took. I am sure there are more shortcuts that I have not listed below. For me, the several shortcuts I took made that day's hike much more enjoyable. It's all about why one does the Appalachian Trail. The easier shortcuts are just plain more enjoyable and may be enough to encourage a distant hiker to keep going, especially a thru-hiker.

*(1) I started out by following the white blazes for the first 400 miles. Leaving Damascus, I stayed on the Creeper Trail for ten miles. The ten miles of the Creeper Trail was next to a cascading stream, which made the hike much more enjoyable. This allowed me to skip a couple of miles of viewless climbs.

(2) After descending the Priest in Virginia and climbing about 800 feet up the next mountain, a hiker will come to a signpost designating the Mau-Har Trail. The Mau-Har Trail is a blue-blaze shortcut to the Maupin Field Shelter. This avoids an extra four miles up a difficult climb and descent over Three Ridges Mountain.

(3) The first climb out of Duncannon, Pa, a hiker will come to the Susquehanna Trail. It is a blue-blaze shortcut to the Clarks Ferry Shelter. This shortcut avoids a time-consuming trek up and over a half-mile boulder maze.

*(4) Leaving the Ten Mile Shelter, shortly after entering Connecticut, a hiker may follow the 16-mile trail and dirt

road along the banks of the beautiful cascading Housatonic River. This again was a most enjoyable hike and avoided many needless climbs and ridiculous descents.

*(5)   There are a couple of Blue-Blazed Trails that skips Stratton Mountain in Vermont. It cuts out about two miles of climbing.

(6)   At the top of Killington Mountain in Vermont, a hiker will come to Jungle Junction. Take the Sherburne Pass Trail. A much shorter trail to Route 4. As you cross Route 4 to The Inn at Long Trail, there is a short climb that takes a hiker back to the AT, then it is about a two mile hike to Mountain Meadows Lodge.

*(7)   Another more enjoyable trail is the Warden's Trail in NH. At about mile 1764.6 northbound, just before climbing Smarts Mountain, a hiker will come to a parking lot. Instead of taking the White-Blazed Trail, continue through the parking lot and take the Warden's Trail. It is a nice trail along a flowing stream. After a couple of miles, you will come to the old warden's garage. Fill your water bottles there. From there, it is a good mile to the AT. Continue the climb on the AT to the summit of Smarts Mountain. (It's a very nice resting spot.)

(8)   Another much more enjoyable hike is the six-mile XYZ trail in NH from the Zeeland Hut to the AMC Highland Center. From there, take a nice gradual four-mile climb back up to the AT on the popular Crawford Path, along another cascading stream.

(9)   From the Lake of the Clouds Hut, a much shorter six-mile hike to Pinkham Notch is to take the popular Tuckerman Ravine Trail, especially in bad weather.

*(10)   From Pinkham Notch, taking the Gondola to the top of Wildcat Mountain is not only enjoyable, but avoids a dangerous and exhausting climb.

*(11) After Saddleback and Junior Saddleback in Maine, a hiker can take a much smoother Caribou Pond Trail for about eight miles, all the way to Route 27. Having the Guthook GPS is necessary in a couple of spots.

*(12) If a hiker stays at the really nice Hostel of Maine on Route 27, by crossing the street, another beautiful seven mile trail called the Narrow Gage Pathway, follows on the banks of another cascading stream and eventually connects with the Maine Hut Trail. Take the Maine Hut Trail north past the Poplar Hut and continue for seven more gradual miles back to the Appalachian Trail (it's a huge shortcut).

(13) Another big shortcut can be found in the 100 Mile Wilderness. At about mile 2094 northbound, the Third Chairback Mountain Trail will take you one and a half miles down to the very nice AMC Gorham Cabin Lodge for the night. The next morning, take the two-mile Iron Works Road back to the AT. This short cut bypasses a very challenging stretch of the Chairback Mountains and could be a lifesaver in bad weather.

(14) There is a short road walk shortcut between miles 2151 and 2153 that avoids a needless climb.

(15) And finally, after leaving Abol and reaching the Baxter Park boundary, there is a much smoother and shorter Blue-Blazed Trail to the base of Katahdin.

Some Recommended Gear

(1) zpack.com – Super lightweight tents, backpacks, and gear
 (a) Plexamid tent, 14.8 oz = $549
 (b) Flat tent groundsheet, 2.5 oz = $85
 (c) Food bag, 1.5 oz = $39
 (d) Arc Haul backpack, 24 oz = $299
 (e) Vertice rain jacket, 5.6 oz = $299
 (f) Variety of sleeping bags

(2) tarptent.com – Great lightweight 30 oz tents = $200

(3) LLBean.com – 2 pairs of Classic Supplex sport shorts = $35 each
(Lightweight, comfortable, and fast drying)

(4) Patagonia.com
 (a) Nano Puff® Hoody = $249
 (b) Capilene short-sleeve T-shirt = $39
 (c) Capilene long-sleeve T-shirt = $49
(Both T-shirts are lightweight and fast drying)

(5) REI.com
    (a) Injinji midweight toe socks (no blisters)
    (b) Darn Tough hiking socks
    (c) Altra Olympus hiking shoes = $150
    (d) Diamondback trail pro shock trekking poles = $139
    (e) Petzl Actik headlamp = $45
    (f) Jetboil Flash Cooking System = $99
    (g) Sawyer mini water filter = $19
    (h) Variety of sleeping bags and pads

(6) Hiking Guides
    (a) *Appalachian Trail Thru-Hikers' Companion* (renewed every year)
    (b) Appalachian Trail guidebook (renewed every year)
    (c) National Geographic Appalachian Trail map books
    (d) Guthook – app for iPhone
    (e) Trailjournals.com